The Marker Family

The Marker Family

of Maryland, Ohio, Iowa, and California

German-Americans Moving West

Carolyn Ladd, CG®

Genealogy House
Amherst, Massachusetts

First published 2023 by Genealogy House,
a division of White River Press, PO Box 3561, Amherst, MA 01004
www. genealogyhouse.net

This book is published for genealogical, educational, and historical purposes.

ISBN: 979-8-88545-001-0

Book and cover design by Douglas Lufkin
Lufkin Graphic Designs, Norwich, Vermont 05055
www.lufkingraphics.com

Library of Congress Cataloging-in-Publication Data

Names: Ladd, Carolyn Helen, 1966- author.
Title: The Marker family of Maryland, Ohio, Iowa, and California : German
   Americans moving west / Carolyn Ladd, CG.
Description: Amherst : Genealogy House, 2023. | Includes bibliographical
   references and index.
Identifiers: LCCN 2023020761 | ISBN 9798885450010 (hardback)
Subjects: LCSH: Marker family. | Marker, George, 1780-1854--Family. |
   German Americans--Genealogy. | United States--Genealogy.
Classification: LCC CS71.M343 2023 | DDC 929.20973--dc23/eng/20230502
LC record available at https://lccn.loc.gov/2023020761

Dedication

This book is dedicated to my parents, John Raymond and Judith Ann (Lenaway) Ladd, who have always supported my interest in genealogy. And to my paternal grandfather, Raymond John Ladd, an oral family historian who first told me about the Marker family.

Contents

Introduction i

Generation One—Martin Marker and Margaret Weaver. 1

Generation Two—Martin Van Buren Marker and Martha Jane Hoover. 36

Generation Three—Harriet Viola Marker and Frank Oscar Ladd 72

Conclusion 91

Marker Family Tree 93

Index 95

Introduction

THE MARKER FAMILY valued family, faith, industriousness, and education. As this German-American family moved west for greater economic opportunities, they stayed connected. Family members moved together and lived near each other; they helped each other in difficult times. Many were active members of churches. They were able to buy land. Some helped establish churches by donating money or land, and some served in positions of leadership. The Marker family worked hard at farming and raising livestock, and they were entrepreneurial in selling land and establishing businesses as they lived the American Dream.

Martin Marker and Margaret Weaver

MARTIN MARKER was born in Frederick County, Maryland, on 15 June 1815 and died on 24 October 1893 in Versailles, Darke County, Ohio.[1] He married **Margaret Weaver** in Montgomery County, Ohio, on 30 March 1837.[2] They were married by Henry Heincke, a German Lutheran minister.[3] Margaret was born on 18 January 1818 in Montgomery County, and died in Versailles on 24 January 1901.[4]

---

1   All websites were accessed as of 21 Nov. 2022. For birth: *The History of Darke County, Ohio, Containing a History of the County; its Cities, Towns, etc.; General and Local Statistics; Portraits of Early Settlers and Prominent Men; History of the Northwest Territory; History of Ohio; Map of Darke County; Constitution of the United States, Miscellaneous Matters, etc., etc.* (Chicago: W. H. Beers & Co., 1880), 612. For death and calculated date of birth: Brock Cemetery (Greenville, St. Mary's Road, Darke Co., Ohio; LAT/LON 40.2598818, -84.5609921), Martin Marker gravestone; read and photographed by author, 17 May 2022. For birth and death: "Death of an Old Pioneer," *Greenville Democrat* (Greenville, Ohio), 1 Nov. 1893, p. 3, col. 4. For date and place of death: Darke County, Ohio, death certificate, vol. 2, p. 154, Martin Marker, 24 Oct. 1893; Probate Court, Greenville.

2   Montgomery County, Ohio, marriage record & certificate, [no vol. no.], p. 161, Marker-Weaver, 30 March 1837; Probate Court, Dayton.

3   Montgomery Co., Marker-Weaver. For denomination of officiant: Dale E. Schmolinsky, *Sesquicentennial Celebration, Trinity United Church of Christ, Miamisburg, Ohio* (no pub. or date of pub.); imaged at Internet Archive (www.archive.org).

4   For birth: *The History of Darke County, Ohio*, 612. For death and calculated date of birth: Brock Cemetery (Greenville, St. Mary's Road, Darke Co., Ohio; LAT/LON 40.2598818, -84.5609921), Margaret Marker gravestone; read and photographed by author, 17 May 2022. For birth and death: obituary for Mrs. Margaret Marker (née Weaver), newspaper unk.; in the collection of the Garst Museum, Greenville, Ohio. For birth location, date and place of death: Darke County, Ohio, death certificate, vol. 2, p. 159, Margaret Marker, 24 Jan. 1901; Probate Court, Greenville.

Martin Marker's Father was George Marker

No birth or christening record was found for Martin Marker.[5] Neither his death record from Darke County, Ohio, nor his obituary named his parents.[6] George Marker is identified as Martin's father in four documents: a deed from 1834, a published biography from 1880, a published biography from 1900, and a booklet from 1964. The deed dated 1834 in Montgomery County, Ohio, from Paul Marker to the "children of George

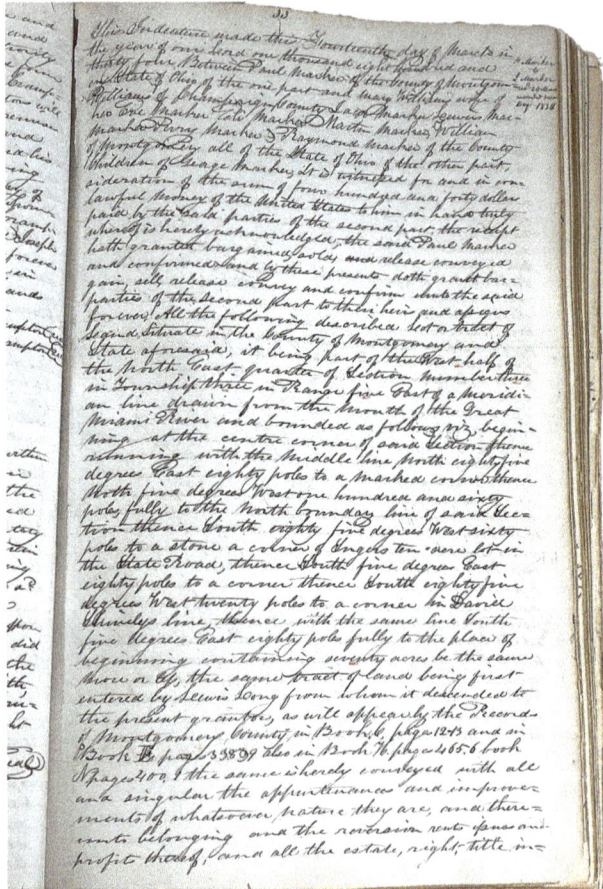

1834 deed from Paul Marker to the "children of George Marker."

---

5 Birth records for Frederick County, Maryland, did not start until 1898. "Frederick County, Maryland Genealogy," FamilySearch (www.familysearch.org/en/wiki/Frederick_County,_Maryland_Genealogy). "Maryland Births and Christenings, 1650–1995," index, and "Maryland, Births and Baptisms, 1665–1995," index, FamilySearch (www.familysearch.org), broad searches for Marker + 1815. "Maryland, U.S., Births and Christenings Index, 1662–1911," index, Ancestry (www.ancestry.com); broad search for Marker + 1815.

6 Darke County, Ohio, death certificate, vol. 2, p. 154, Martin Marker, 24 Oct. 1893; Probate Court, Greenville. "Death of an Old Pioneer," *Greenville Democrat*, 1 Nov. 1893.

Marker," named those children as Mary Williams (wife of William Williams), Jacob Marker, Lewis Marker, Ezra Marker, Eli Marker, Martin Marker, William Marker, Perry Marker, and Raymond Marker.[7] Paul Marker was probably George Marker's brother.[8]

A biography of Martin Marker in *The History of Darke County, Ohio*, dated 1880, reports that George Marker of Frederick County, Maryland, was the father of Martin Marker,[9] and that Martin's mother was George's wife named Margaret, but does not give her maiden name.[10] Adding to the credibility of the information, the unnamed author apparently interviewed Martin Marker for the biography, writing: "He relates many thrilling incidents of his early life in Darke Co., which the writer would have been pleased to mention, but, for the want of space, had to omit." Also, Martin Marker was still alive when the biography was published in 1880.

A 1900 biography of George E. Marker, grandson of George Marker and son of Ezra Marker, says that Ezra's father was George Marker and his mother was Margaret Storm.[11] Ezra was Martin Marker's brother.[12]

In addition, a booklet published in 1964, celebrating the sesquicentennial of Versailles, Ohio, includes this entry about the Marker family: "George Marker was born January 19, 1780. He was married to Margaret Sturm in 1801. To this union 11 children were born, including: Jacob, Mary, Lewis, Ezra, Elim, Martin, William, Perry, Raymon."[13]

---

7   Montgomery County, Ohio, Deed Record S:33–34, from Paul Marker and his wife, Eliza, to the children of George Marker, 14 March 1834; Montgomery County Archives, Dayton.

8   Neil D. Thompson, "George Marker Sr. of Frederick County, Maryland," *The Genealogist 1* (Spring 1980): 98–101.

9   *The History of Darke County, Ohio*, 612.

10 *The History of Darke County, Ohio*, 612.

11 *A Biographical History of Darke County, Ohio: Compendium of National Biography* (Chicago: Lewis Publishing Company, 1900), 573–574.

12 Montgomery County, Ohio, Deed Record S:33–34.

13 *1814–1964 150 Years of Progress, Sesquicentennial Celebration, Versailles, Ohio* (Versailles, Ohio: Sesquicentennial Historical Committee, 1964), 78. The booklet does not name their two children who died in infancy.

George Marker died on 29 November 1854 and is buried in the Ellerton Cemetery in Montgomery County, Ohio.[14] No will or probate file was found for him.[15]

George Marker's Gravestone, Ellerton Cemetery,
Montgomery County, Ohio.

Martin Marker's Mother was Margaret (Storm) Marker

Margaret Storm was the daughter of Michael and Magdalena Storm. She was born on 13 April 1783 and was baptized on 8 June 1783 at the German Reformed Church of Frederick, Maryland.[16] George Marker and Margaret Storm were issued a marriage license in Frederick County, Maryland, on 12 May 1801;[17] their marriage on 13 May

---

14   Ellerton Cemetery (Union Road, Montgomery Co., Ohio; LAT/LON 39.6798615, -84.3098243), George Marker gravestone; read and photographed by author, 18 May 2022.

15   "Court Records 1805–1910, and Indexes 1803–1939, Montgomery County, Ohio," digital images, FamilySearch (www.familysearch.org) > Film # 005876864 > image 105 of 655; Administrator's and Executor's General Index 1803–1894, p. 179; Montgomery County Probate Court, Dayton. Lindsay M. Brien, *An Index of Wills and Administrations, Montgomery County, Ohio, 1803–1893* (Salt Lake City, Utah: Genealogy Society, 1954), 57–58. (No listing for Marker.)

16   "Transcript of Church Records, 1747–1875 [Evangelical Reformed]," digital images, FamilySearch (www.familysearch.org) > Film # 007575962 > image 779 of 1366, Baptism of Margaret Storm, 8 June 1783; vol. 1, p. 182; citing Maryland Historical Society, Baltimore, Md.

17   Frederick County, Maryland, Index to Marriages 1778–1886, p. 244; Clerk of the Circuit Court for Frederick County, Frederick.

1801 was recorded in German in the records of the Evangelical Lutheran Church of Frederick, Maryland.[18] ("Sturm" means "storm" in German.[19])

The Evangelical Lutheran Church of Frederick, Maryland, was founded in 1738 by Germans who migrated from Pennsylvania to Maryland in search of farmland.[20] For the first sixty years, church records were kept in German.[21] Services were conducted in German until 1816 when a new pastor began conducting services in English to appeal to young people.[22] The church is still open and operating today.[23]

Margaret (Storm) Marker died on 12 February 1870. Her death notice appeared in a Preble County, Ohio, newspaper.

—On the 12th inst., at the residence of her son, Lewis Marker, on Banta's Creek, Mrs MARGARET MARKER, aged 86 years, 9 months and 29 days. After a long and useful life she rests from her labors

Margaret Marker's Death Notice from *Eaton Weekly Register*
(Eaton, Ohio), 24 Feb. 1870, p. 3, col. 1.

Margaret is buried in the Sugar Hill German Baptist Cemetery in Preble County, Ohio. Her gravestone reads: "Margaret wife of George Marker, Died February 12, 1870."[24] She is buried near her son Lewis who died on 24 July 1892.[25] Lewis Marker's obituary says that he was "a brother to Ezra and Martin Marker, of Versailles, two of our oldest citizens."[26]

---

18   Evangelical Lutheran Church (Frederick, Maryland), Historic Parish Records, vol. I, p. 320, Marker–Sturm, 13 May 1801.

19   "Sturm Family History," Ancestry (www.ancestry.com/name-origin?surname=sturm).

20   Abdel Ross Wentz, *History of the Evangelical Lutheran Church of Frederick Maryland 1738–1938* (Harrisburg, Pa.: Evangelical Press 1938), p. 20.

21   Wentz, *History of the Evangelical Lutheran Church of Frederick Maryland,* 177.

22   Wentz, *History of the Evangelical Lutheran Church of Frederick Maryland,* 177.

23   "Evangelical Lutheran Church," (www.twinspires.org: accessed 7 Oct. 2022).

24   Sugar Hill German Baptist Cemetery (Highway 35, Preble Co., Ohio; LAT/LON 39.7442300, -84.5175036), Margaret Marker gravestone; read and photographed by author, 18 May 2022.

25   Sugar Hill German Baptist Cemetery (Highway 35, Preble Co., Ohio; LAT/LON 39.7442300, -84.5175036), "Louis" Marker gravestone; read and photographed by author, 18 May 2022.

26   "Versailles Items," *Darke County Democratic Advocate* (Greenville, Ohio), 28 July 1892, p. 1, col. 3.

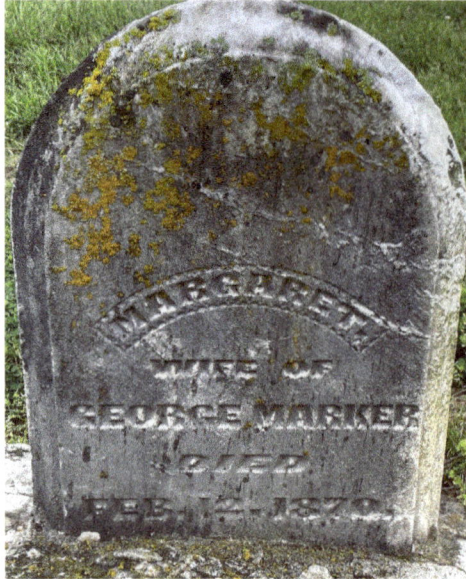

Margaret (Storm) Marker's Gravestone,
Sugar Hill Cemetery, Preble County, Ohio.

The 1900 biography of George E. Marker reports: "George Marker was born in Maryland and was there married to Margaret Storm, who had emigrated thither from Germany, where she was a member of a wealthy farmer, whose estate in the fatherland is yet to be divided among the descendants."[27] Margaret Storm was likely born in Maryland, not Germany. She was baptized at the age of 2 months in Maryland.[28] The 1860 U.S. Census lists her place of birth as Maryland.[29] The biography was published 30 years after Margaret's death; she likely spoke German given that the church where she was baptized and married was conducted in German. It may be that George E. Marker did not know his grandmother's birthplace and assumed it was Germany.

---

27   *A Biographical History of Darke County, Ohio: Compendium of National Biography*, 573–574.

28   "Transcript of Church Records, 1747–1875 [Evangelical Reformed]," digital images, FamilySearch, Baptism of Margaret Storm, 8 June 1783.

29   1860 U.S. Census, Preble County, Ohio, pop. sched., Twin Township, p. 19 (handwritten), dwelling 146, family 143, Margaret Marker in William Marker household; imaged at Ancestry (www.ancestry.com); citing National Archives and Records Administration microfilm publication M653, roll 1026.

Margaret Weaver's Father was John Jacob Weaver

Margaret Weaver, wife of Martin Marker, was the daughter of John Jacob Weaver. He is sometimes referred to in records as John Jacob and sometimes as Jacob because of German naming patterns for boys. German boys were often baptized with the first name Johannes (or John in English). [30] "The second name, known as the *Rufname*, along with the surname is what would be used in marriage, tax, land and death records."[31]

Margaret Marker was named in John Jacob Weaver's will as one of his children. Children named in his will were: Catharine Marker, Margaret Marker, Anna Maria Windbigler, Eve Elizabeth Bertram, Sarah Weaver, Lucinda Shade, Elias Weaver, and Hannah Stine (deceased).[32] In John Jacob Weaver's probate file, Margaret Marker and her husband, Martin Marker, acknowledged receipt of money from her father's estate.[33]

Margaret Weaver's Mother was Susannah (Gebhart) Weaver

Margaret Weaver was born in on 18 January 1818 in Montgomery County, Ohio, before Ohio began keeping birth records.[34] Neither her death record from Darke County, Ohio, nor her newspaper obituary lists her parents.[35] The following documents connect Susannah Gebhart to her husband, John Jacob Weaver; they connect John Jacob Weaver to his children; and they connect Susannah (Gebhart)

---

30 Diane Hadid, "German Naming Traditions Genealogists Should Know," *FamilyTree* magazine (familytreemagazine.com/names/first-names/german-naming-traditions/). "Johannes," Wikipedia (en.wikipedia.org/wiki/Johannes).

31 Hadid, "German Naming Traditions Genealogists Should Know."

32 "Ohio, U.S., Wills and Probate Records, 1786–1998," database with images, Ancestry (www.ancestry.com) > Montgomery County > Will Records, vol. E–G, 1850–1868 > images 967–969 of 1001; Will of John Jacob Weaver, vol. G, pgs. 539–542, written 31 July 1867, proved 12 March 1868; citing Montgomery County Probate Court, Dayton.

33 "Ohio, U.S., Wills and Probate Records, 1786–1998," database with images, Ancestry (www.ancestry.com) > Montgomery County > Probate Files, 9066–9086, 1850–1900 > images 371, 372 of 518, No. 9080, John Jacob Weaver; citing Montgomery County Probate Court, Dayton.

34 For Margaret Weaver's date and place of birth: *The History of Darke County, Ohio*, 612. For calculated birthdate: Brock Cemetery (Darke Co., Ohio), Margaret Marker gravestone. For birth and death: obituary for Mrs. Margaret Marker (née Weaver), newspaper unk.; in the collection of the Garst Museum, Greenville, Ohio. Ohio did not begin recording births until 1867. Diane VanSkriver Gagel, *NGS Research in the States Series, Ohio* (Arlington, Va.: National Genealogical Society, 2008), 46.

35 Darke County, Ohio, death certificate, vol. 2, p. 159, Margaret Marker, 24 Jan. 1901; Probate Court, Greenville. Obituary for Mrs. Margaret Marker (née Weaver), newspaper unk.; in the collection of the Garst Museum, Greenville, Ohio.

Weaver to three of her daughters—Anna Maria Windbigler, Catharine Marker, and Margaret Marker:

- Jacob Weaver and Susannah "Gephart" were married in Montgomery County, Ohio, on 8 December 1814 by a minister of the German Lutheran Church.[36]

- George Gebhart's will written on 15 August 1852 leaves a bequest to daughter "Susanna intermarried with Jacob Weaver," and also names Jacob Weaver as one of the executors.[37]

- Ann Maria Weaver and Samuel Windbigler were married in Montgomery County, Ohio, on 18 October 1838 by German Lutheran Minister Henry Heincke. Present at the marriage was Anna Maria's mother, Susannah Weaver.[38]

- Jacob Weaver died on 6 March 1868.[39] His will lists his wife as Susannah Weaver and lists among his children Margaret Marker, Catharine Marker, and Anna Maria Windbigler.[40]

- Jacob Weaver's obituary from 1868 reports that a few years after moving to Ohio in 1806, he married "Miss Gebhart."[41]

---

36 "Ohio, U.S., County Marriage Records, 1774–1993," database with images, Ancestry (www.ancestry.com) > Montgomery County > 1803–1851 > image 25 of 1114, Weaver-Gephart, 8 Dec. 1814, [no vol.], 46; citing Montgomery County Courthouse, Dayton.

37 "Ohio Probate Records, 1789–1996," database with images, FamilySearch (www.familysearch.org) > Montgomery County > Wills 1850–1868, vols. E–G > image 159 of 1001; citing Montgomery County Probate Court, Dayton; Will of George Gebhart, written 15 Aug, 1852, proved 13 Oct, 1854. Children of George Gebhart listed in the will: Joseph Gebhart, Jacob Gebhart, George Gebhart, Peter Gebhart, David Gebhart (dec'd.), Sarah (wife of Thomas Kreitzer), Susanna (wife of Jacob Weaver), Catharine (wife of John Long), Magdalena (widow of Phillip Weaver), Elizabeth (wife of Jon Shell), and July Ann Kimmel (dec'd.).

38 "Ohio, County Marriages, 1789–2016," database with images, FamilySearch (www.familysearch.org) > Montgomery County > Marriage Records 1838–1844 > image 66 of 212, vol. A2, p. 36, Weaver-Windbigler, 18 Oct. 1838; citing Montgomery County Courthouse, Dayton.

39 Ellerton Cemetery (Union Road, Montgomery Co., Ohio; LAT/LON 39.6798615, -84.3098243), John Jacob Weaver gravestone; read and photographed by author, 18 May 2022.

40 "Ohio, U.S., Wills and Probate Records, 1786–1998," database with images, Ancestry, Will of John Jacob Weaver, Montgomery County Probate Court.

41 "Brief Mention of a Pioneer," *Dayton Daily Journal* (Dayton, Ohio), 17 March 1868, p. 1, col. 3.

- In the 1880 U.S. Census, "Susanah" Weaver was enumerated as living with her daughter "Mariah" Windbigler.[42]

- Susannah Weaver died on 13 April 1884. Her gravestone indicates that she was the wife of J. Weaver.[43]

- Catharine Marker died on 17 February 1898. Her obituary says that her parents' names were John J. and Susannah Weaver, and that she married Ezra Marker on 2 October 1834.[44]

- Margaret Marker died on 24 January 1901. Her obituary does not name her parents, but does refer to her as "Mrs. Margaret Marker (née Weaver)."[45]

- A published genealogy of the Gebhart family lists Susannah (Gebhart) Weaver as the mother of Margaret (Weaver) Marker.[46]

Life of Martin Marker & Margaret Weaver

George Marker moved his family from Frederick County, Maryland, to Montgomery County, Ohio, in about 1823, reportedly after having lost his fortune in Maryland.[47] The family traveled "overland via wagon" and moved onto land that was "practically wilderness."[48] They may have traveled at least in part on The National Road that started in Cumberland, Maryland, and by 1818, extended to Wheeling, Virginia.[49] The family worked hard to clear "howling wilderness" land to create a farm.[50]

---

42 1880 U.S. Census, Darke County, Ohio, pop. sched., York Township, enumeration district 75, p. 417 (stamped), dwelling 167, family 176, Susanah Weaver in the household of Mariah Windbigler; imaged at Ancestry (www.ancestry.com); citing National Archives and Records Administration microfilm publication T9, roll 1011.

43 Find a Grave, digital images (www.findagrave.com), memorial 101421542, Susannah Gebhart Weaver, photographs by "DJMonnier;" citing Brock Cemetery, Darke Co., Ohio.

44 Obituary for Catharine Marker, newspaper unk.; in the collection of the Garst Museum, Greenville, Ohio.

45 Obituary for Mrs. Margaret Marker (née Weaver), newspaper unk.; in the collection of the Garst Museum, Greenville, Ohio.

46 Julia Shupert Hagwood, *Gebhart, Gephart, and Related Families, 1609–1996* (Dayton, Ohio: Epic Printing Works, 1996), 29.

47 *A Biographical History of Darke County, Ohio: Compendium of National Biography*, 573–574.

48 *A Biographical History of Darke County, Ohio: Compendium of National Biography*, 573–574.

49 "National Road," FamilySearch (www.familysearch.org/en/wiki/National_Road). Construction of The National Road, now Highway 40, reached across the state of Ohio by 1838.

50 "Obituary, William Marker," *Dayton Daily Journal* (Dayton, Ohio), 5 Jan. 1905, p. 6, col. 6.

Map of Ohio in 1820 from A. Bourne and J. Kilbourne, *Map of the State of Ohio* (Worcester: American Antiquarian Society, 1820); imaged at the *David Rumsey Map Collection* (www.davidrumsey.com).

In 1830, the George Marker family lived in Perry Township.[51] Perry was settled mostly by Germans who came from Pennsylvania.[52] The early settlers faced many obstacles upon arrival in Ohio, including setting up basic log cabins on land with trees that had to be cut down before crops could be planted.[53] Pioneer women worked long days helping with crops by sowing, planting, and harvesting; providing food to the family by cooking, baking, and making cheese and butter; and providing the family with clothing by operating a spinning wheel and a loom, sewing, and knitting.[54]

Martin Marker "received his education in the subscription schools of Montgomery Co."[55] A schoolhouse was built out of logs in Perry Township in 1814, and parents paid a fee for their children to attend school in either money, produce, or by providing housing to the teacher.[56]

In 1837, when he was about 22 years old, tax records show that Martin Marker owned four horses worth $160.[57] He lived in Jefferson Township in Montgomery County, Ohio.[58] Jefferson Township was founded in 1804 almost entirely by German Lutherans.[59]

Martin Marker and Margaret Weaver married in Montgomery County, Ohio, on 30 March 1837.[60] They were married by Henry Heincke, a German Lutheran minister.[61]

---

51   1830 U.S. Census, Montgomery County, Ohio, pop. sched., Perry Township, p. 296 (handwritten), George Marker household; imaged at Ancestry (www.ancestry.com); citing National Archives and Records Administration microfilm publication M19, roll 136.

52   David A. Puderbaugh, ed., *Montgomery County History and Annual,* 3 vols. (Dayton, Ohio: Christian Publishing Association, 1926), 1:161.

53   Puderbaugh, ed., *Montgomery County History and Annual,* 1:161.

54   H. A. Rattermann, *German Pioneers of Montgomery County, Ohio* (Baltimore, Md.: Genealogical Publishing Company, 2014), 17–18.

55   *The History of Darke County, Ohio,* 612.

56   Puderbaugh, *Montgomery County History and Annual,* 1:161.

57   "Ohio Tax Records, 1800–1850," database with images, FamilySearch (www.familysearch.org) > Film # 004849488 > image 368 of 692; vol. 1837, Jefferson Township, pgs. 63–64; citing Montgomery County Courthouse, Dayton, Ohio.

58   "Ohio Tax Records, 1800–1850," pps. 63–64.

59   Rattermann, *German Pioneers of Montgomery County, Ohio,* 8.

60   Montgomery County, Ohio, marriage record, [no vol. no.], 161, Marker-Weaver, 30 March 1837; Montgomery County Probate Court, Dayton. *The History of Darke County, Ohio,* 612.

61   Schmolinsky, *Sesquicentennial Celebration, Trinity United Church of Christ, Miamisburg, Ohio.*

Interestingly, Margaret's sister Catharine Weaver and Martin's brother Ezra Marker were married about two and a half years prior also by Henry Heincke.[62]

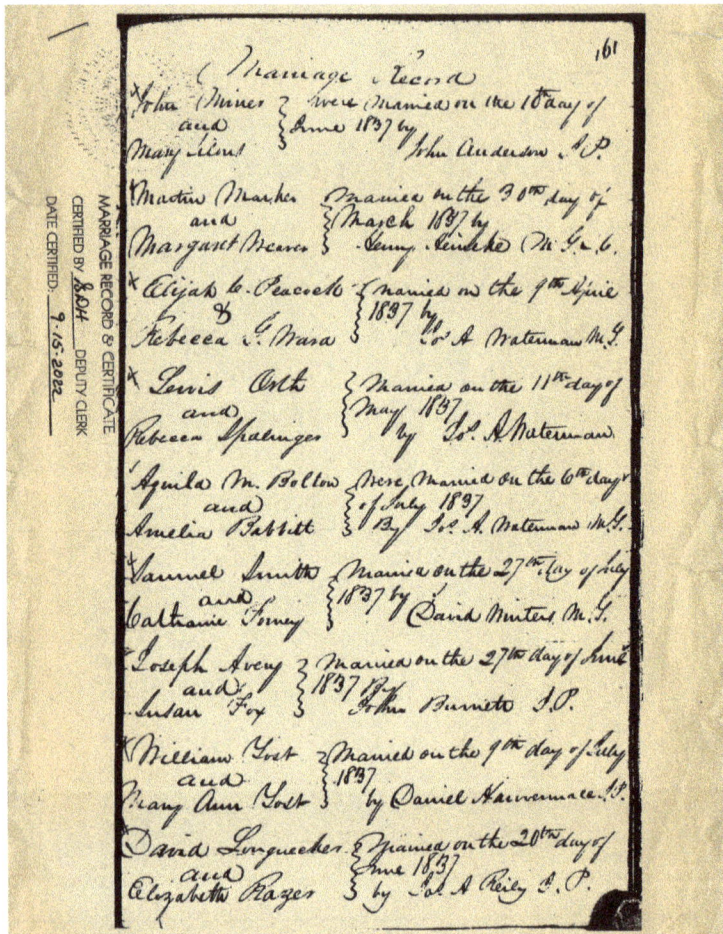

Marriage record of Margaret Weaver and Martin Marker.

In 1838, Martin owned one horse worth $40 and two cattle worth $16.[63] Martin and Margaret had their first child on 12 February 1838, a daughter named Lavina.[64]

---

62 "Ohio, U.S., County Marriage Records, 1774–1993," database with images, Ancestry (www.ancestry .com) > Montgomery County > 1803–1851 > image 146 of 1114, p. 106, Marker-Weaver, 2 Oct. 1834; citing Montgomery County Courthouse, Dayton.

63 "Ohio Tax Records, 1800–1850," database with images, FamilySearch (www.familysearch.org) > Film # 004849498 > image 426 of 813; vol. 1838, Jefferson Township, pps. 77–78; citing Montgomery County Courthouse, Dayton, Ohio.

64 *The History of Darke County, Ohio*, 612.

The next year, Martin lived in Butler Township in Montgomery County, and owned three horses worth $120 and two cattle worth $16.[65]

By 1840, the young family lived in York Township in Darke County, Ohio, on property given to them by Margaret's father.[66] York Township was formed in 1837, and many of the early families were Germans who had immigrated to Ohio from Pennsylvania.[67] Martin "erected a log cabin and began the laborious task of opening up a farm; he cleared and put under cultivation about 40 acres."[68] In 1840, the household consisted of one male under the age of 5, one male between the ages of 20 and 30, one female under the age of 5, and one female between the ages of 20 and 30.[69] Those likely were Martin, Margaret, their daughter Lavina, and their son Martin Van Buren, who was born on 27 June 1840.[70]

President Martin Van Buren, a Democrat, was inaugurated in 1837.[71] Martin Van Buren Marker was born in 1840 while Martin Van Buren was president of the United States.[72] It may be that Martin Marker named his son Martin Van Buren Marker in honor of the president. Martin Marker was a Democrat and ran for land appraiser on the Democratic ticket in 1852.[73] He served as the appraiser and platted and appraised the lands in five townships in Darke County.[74] Martin also was active in the Democratic party.[75] President Van Buren was a one-term president (1837–1841), as he was not reelected. Notable facts about President Van Buren:

---

65 "Ohio Tax Records, 1800–1850," database with images, FamilySearch (www.familysearch.org) > Film # 004849499 > image 339 of 687; vol. 1839, Butler Township, pps. 696–697; citing Montgomery County Courthouse, Dayton, Ohio.

66 *The History of Darke County, Ohio*, 612.

67 *The History of Darke County, Ohio*, 408.

68 *The History of Darke County, Ohio*, 612.

69 1840 U.S. Census, Darke County, Ohio, pop. sched., York Township, [no p.], Martin Marker household; imaged at Ancestry (www.ancestry.com); citing National Archives and Records Administration microfilm publication M704, roll 390.

70 For Martin Van Buren Marker's date of birth: California Department of Public Health, death certificate no. 22-030921, Martin Van Buren Marker, 8 July 1922; Bureau of Vital Statistics, Sacramento.

71 Bernard Grun, *The Timetables of History, A Horizontal Linkage of People and Events*, 4th ed. (New York: Simon & Schuster, 2005), 402.

72 "Martin Van Buren, 8th President of the United States," The White House (www.whitehouse.gov/about-the-white-house/presidents/martin-van-buren/).

73 "Death of an Old Pioneer," *Greenville Democrat*, 1 Nov. 1893. "Democratic Ticket," *Greenville Telegraph* (Greenville, Ohio), 1 Oct. 1852, p. 2, col. 1.

74 *The History of Darke County, Ohio*, 612.

75 "For the Telegraph," *Greenville Telegraph*, 18 Feb. 1853, p. 2, col. 4.

- He was the first president who was born an American.

- He opposed annexing Texas as a slave state.[76]

- He was president during the most severe economic depression to hit the U.S. at that time. Called "The Great Panic," it began in 1837; banks closed, businesses failed, and some people lost their land. President Van Buren was criticized for not intervening in the failing economy.[77]

Voters of the state of Ohio where the Markers lived had not elected Van Buren in the 1836 election, but had voted for Whig William H. Harrison.[78]

In 1848, one of the first churches was built in York Township on land that Martin Marker's brother Ezra deeded to the Lutheran and German Reform trustees for $5.00.[79] The first railroad came to Darke County in 1853; one train—mixed passenger and freight—ran each day.[80]

By 1850, Martin Marker was 35 years old, married, and he and Margaret had five children living at home: Lavina, age 11; Martin, age 9; Mary, age 6; Manuel, age 4; and Cornelius, age 2.[81] Living and farming in Wayne Township, Darke County, Martin had 105 acres of improved land and 65 of unimproved land; his farm was worth $4,000. He owned 3 horses, 4 milch cows, 2 other cattle, 27 sheep, and 22 swine worth $237. His farm produced 60 pounds of wool, 10 pounds of potatoes, 20 bushels of buckwheat, 150 pounds of butter, 5 tons of hay, and 60 bushels of flaxseed in the prior year.[82] On 4 July 1850, Martin and Margaret Marker hosted a 4th of July celebration at their "beautiful residence" near Jacksonville, Ohio. An attorney gave

---

76   "Martin Van Buren, 8th President of the United States," The White House.

77   "Panic of 1837," The Library of Congress (www.americaslibrary.gov/aa/buren/aa_buren_panic_1.html).

78   Dave Leip, "1836 Presidential Election Results," *Atlas of U.S. Presidential Elections* (http://uselectionatlas. org/RESULTS/national.php?year=1836).

79   *The History of Darke County, Ohio*, 612. Darke County, Ohio, Deed Book R1: 138, Ezra Marker and wife Catharine to Samuel Windbeigher and Samuel Sherry as trustees for the Lutheran and German Reform, 27 Dec. 1847; Recorder's Office, Greenville.

80   *The History of Darke County, Ohio*, 328–329. Sesquicentennial Celebration, Versailles, Ohio, 23.

81   1850 U.S. Census, Darke County, Ohio, pop. sched., Wayne Township, p. 308 (stamped), dwelling 83, family 83, Martin Marker household; imaged at Ancestry (www.ancestry.com); citing National Archives and Records Administration microfilm publication M432, roll 674.

82   1850 U.S. Census, Darke County, Ohio, agricultural schedule, p. 53, Martin Marker; imaged at Ancestry (www.ancestry.com); citing National Archives and Records Administration microfilm publication T1159, roll 2.

an oration, and attendees were treated to "the delicacies, extras, and substantials of the country."[83]

Sadly, Martin's brother Raymond died in Darke County on 9 November 1855 at the age of 34.[84] Raymond's wife, Eliza, had died eleven months prior on 18 January 1855 at the age of 28.[85] Eliza's death may have been related to childbirth because their daughter Lucinda died a week after her mother at the age of 2 months and 18 days.[86] The three share a common gravestone at the Greenlawn Cemetery in Versailles, Darke County. Raymond's inscription is in German; his wife's and his daughter's inscriptions are in English. Raymond and Eliza left behind four orphaned children: Leonard, age 9; Allen, age 7; Hiram, age 5; and Margaret Catharine, age 4.[87]

Raymond Marker's siblings pitched in to help the orphans. Martin Marker served as the legal guardian and received court permission to sell the real estate owned by Raymond at a public auction, and to put the money in trust for the children.[88] Brother Ezra Marker was the highest bidder and bought Raymond's property for $4,328.[89] Brother Perry Marker took in Leonard and Hiram.[90] Sister Mary (Marker) Williams took in Margaret.[91] Allen also remained in Darke County, although whom

---

83 *Democratic Herald* (Greenville, Ohio), 10 July 1850, p. 2, col. 1.

84 Find a Grave, digital images (www.findagrave.com), memorial 133323715 for Raymund John Marker, photographs by "DJMonnier;" citing Greenlawn Cemetery, Darke Co., Ohio.

85 Find a Grave, digital image (www.findagrave.com), memorial 133166984 for Eliza Bachman Marker, photograph by "DJMonnier;" citing Greenlawn Cemetery, Darke Co., Ohio.

86 Find a Grave, digital images (www.findagrave.com), memorial 133167061 for Lucinda Marker, photographs by "DJMonnier;" citing Greenlawn Cemetery, Darke Co., Ohio.

87 "Ohio, Darke County, Probate Records, 1818–1910," digital images, FamilySearch (www.familysearch.org) > Film # 007712588 > images 539–545 of 977, Civil Record, vol. A (1852–1857), no. 1102, pps. 359–372, Guardian of Marker's Heirs, 1855–1856; Probate Court, Greenville.

88 "Ohio, Darke County, Probate Records, 1818–1910," digital images, FamilySearch (www.familysearch.org) > Film # 005492066 > image 526 of 865, Civil Journal, vol. A (1852–1856), p. 562, Petition to Sell Lands, 14 Jan. 1856; Probate Court, Greenville.

89 "Ohio, Darke County, Probate Records, 1818–1910," digital images, FamilySearch (www.familysearch.org) > Film # 007712588 > images 539–545 of 977, Civil Record, vol. A (1852–1857), no. 1102, pps. 359–372, Guardian of Marker's Heirs, 1855–1856; Probate Court, Greenville.

90 1860 U.S. Census, Montgomery County, pop. sched., Jefferson Township, p. 3 (handwritten), dwelling 19, family 19, Leonard Marker and Hiram Marker in Perry Marker household; imaged at Ancestry (www.ancestry.com); citing National Archives and Records Administration microfilm publication M653, roll 1013. *A Biographical History of Darke County, Ohio: Compendium of National Biography*, 622.

91 1860 U.S. Census, Champaign County, Ohio, pop. sched., Johnson Township, pps. 36– 37 (handwritten), dwelling 587, family 587, M.C. Marker in the William Williams household; imaged at Ancestry (www.ancestry.com); citing National Archives and Records Administration microfilm publication M653, roll 942.

he lived with is unknown.[92] As an adult, Leonard became a cabinetmaker and then a maker of custom coffins and an undertaker in Versailles, Ohio. He buried over 6,000 people during his fifty-year career.[93]

Between 1850 and 1860, the value of Martin Marker's farmland increased and he obtained more livestock. In 1860, Martin Marker lived in Wayne Township, Darke County, was 45 years old, and was living with Margaret and seven children in the home: Martin, age 22; Mary, age 16; Emanuel, age 14; Martha J., age 8; twins Lucinda, age 5, and Malinda, age 5; and Josiah, age 2.[94] Martin was farming 130 acres of improved land, 30 acres of unimproved land, and his farm was worth $5,000. He owned 7 horses, 7 milch cows, 2 other cattle, 30 sheep, and 33 swine, for a total worth of $900. His farm produced 433 bushels of wheat, 40 bushels of rye, 1,000 bushels of corn, 400 bushels of oats, 80 pounds of wool, 40 pounds of potatoes, 70 bushels of barley, 520 pounds of butter, 8 tons of hay, 115 bushels of flaxseed, and 15 gallons of maple syrup in the prior year.[95]

Martin Marker moved from Darke County, Ohio, to Cedar County, Iowa, in 1864. Cedar County is located in eastern Iowa and is over 400 miles from Darke County.[96] Martin Marker first purchased land in Cedar County, Iowa, on 30 January 1864, when he purchased 325 acres for which he paid $6,500 in cash.[97] The deed lists him as "Martin Marker of Darke County, State of Ohio." He made another purchase of 20 acres on 2 May 1864 for $300, and that deed lists him as "Martin Marker now of the

---

92 A document in the probate file says that Allen Marker son of Raymond Marker still resided in Darke Co., Ohio. "Ohio, Darke County, Probate Records, 1818–1910," digital images, FamilySearch (www.familysearch .org) > Film # 007712588 > image 540 of 977, Civil Record, vol. A (1852–1857), no. 1102, p. 540, Petition to Sell Land, 14 Jan. 1856; Probate Court, Greenville. Allen Marker was not found in the 1860 U.S. Census. "1860 United States Federal Census," database with images, Ancestry (www.ancestry.com) searches for Allen + Marker + Ohio and Marker + Darke County, Ohio. Also, each of Raymond Marker's siblings' entries in the 1860 U.S. census was reviewed.

93 *The History of Darke County, Ohio*, 611. *A Biographical History of Darke County, Ohio: Compendium of National Biography*, 623. "Great Community Leader was the Late Leonard Marker . . . Well Known Funeral Director," [newspaper unk.]; in the collection of the Garst Museum, Greenville, Ohio.

94 1860 U.S. Census, Darke County, Ohio, pop. sched., Wayne Township, p. 254 (stamped), dwelling 1789, family 1795, Martin Marker household; imaged at Ancestry (www.ancestry.com); citing National Archives and Records Administration microfilm publication M653, roll 956.

95 1860 U.S. Census, Darke County, Ohio, agricultural schedule, p. 57, Martin Marker, imaged at Ancestry (www.ancestry.com); citing National Archives and Records Administration microfilm publication T1159, roll 18.

96 Google Maps, directions from Darke Co., Ohio, to Cedar Co., Iowa (www.google.com/maps).

97 Cedar County, Iowa, Deed Book T:255–256, William Bandeen and his wife, Jane, to Martin Marker, date of instrument 30 Jan. 1864, date of filing 30 Jan. 1864; Recorder's Office, Tipton.

county of Cedar and the state of Iowa."[98] Presumably he moved from Ohio to Iowa sometime after 30 January 1864 and before 2 May 1864.

Martin Marker and his older brother, Eli Marker, lived near each other in Darke County.[99] Eli also moved to Cedar County about a year after Martin. On 28 February 1865, Eli purchased 140 acres for $5,000 in Cedar County near the land that Martin had purchased.[100] Eli remained in Cedar County for the rest of his life.[101] He died on 27 October 1874 and is buried at Sand Hill Cemetery with his wife, Catherine.[102]

Eli and Catherine Marker Gravestones, Sand Hill Cemetery, Tipton, Iowa.

---

98   Cedar County, Iowa, Deed Book T:637, William Mason (Guardian of James A. Johnson, a minor) to Martin Marker, date of instrument 12 May 1864, date of filing 20 May 1864; Recorder's Office, Tipton.

99   For sibling relationship: Montgomery County, Ohio, Deed Record S:33, from Paul Marker to the children of George Marker, 14 March 1834; Montgomery County Archives, Dayton. Martin and Eli were enumerated on the same page of the 1860 census in Darke County. 1860 U.S. Census, Darke County, Ohio, pop. sched., Wayne Township, p. 254 (handwritten), for Martin Marker household dwelling 1789, family 1795; for Eli Marker household dwelling 1795, family 1801; imaged at Ancestry (www.ancestry.com); citing National Archives and Records Administration microfilm publication M653, roll 956.

100 Cedar County, Iowa, Deed Book V:10–11, Henry Horn & Ann his wife to Eli Marker, date of instrument 28 Feb. 1865, date of filing 28 Feb. 1865; Recorder's Office, Tipton. Both properties purchased by Martin and Eli were in Township 81 North, Range 3 West of the 5th Principal Meridian.

101 1870 U.S. Census, Cedar County, Iowa, pop. sched., Cass Township, pps. 130–131 (stamped), dwelling 21, family 21, Eli Marker household; imaged at Ancestry (www.ancestry.com); citing National Archives and Records Administration microfilm publication M593, roll 380.

102 Sand Hill Cemetery (Jefferson Avenue, Cedar Co., Iowa; LAT/LON 41.7903573, -91.1810993), Eli Marker and Catharine Marker gravestones; read and photographed by author, 6 June 2022. "Iowa, U.S., Wills and Probate Records, 17588–1997," database with images, Ancestry (www.ancestry.com) > Cedar > Case Nos. 1139–1169 (1833–1898) > Case No. 1149, Eli Marker > image 783 of 1596.

While living in Cedar County, Iowa, Martin Marker was an enterprising real estate investor. In August 1865, he purchased 120 acres of timberland in Section 13 of Linn Township in Cedar County for $5,200.[103] He had that timberland surveyed and subdivided into 5-acre lots, which then he sold in 13 sales to 15 buyers between August 1865 and September 1866.[104]

Table 1:	Sales of Timberland in Cedar County, Iowa in Section 13 of Linn Township by Martin Marker & Margaret his Wife		
Purchaser	**Date of Sale**	**Acres**	**Price**
George Galbraith	12 August 1865	5	$500[a]
Alexander Moffett	12 August 1865	10	$900[b]
Thomas & Frances Moffett	12 August 1865	10	$500[c]
Martin V. Marker	12 August 1865	10	$400[d]
William Moffett	12 September 1865	15	$850[e]
Richard Jackson	25 October 1865	5	$312.50[f]
George Boomershine	3 November 1865	10	$294*[g]
George & John Potter	1 January 1866	5	$375[h]
Conrad Miller	2 February 1866	10	$200[i]
Christopher Stotler	17 February 1866	10	$750[j]
Baldwin Parsons	7 April 1866	5	$370[k]
Richard Jackson	18 September 1866	5	$100[l]
Robert Maxwell	21 September 1866	20	$769**[m]

*   sold in combination with 80 acres from Sec. 18, Twp 81, R 3; used average price per acre
**   sold in combination with 240 acres from Sec. 17 & 18, Twp 81, R 3; used average price per acre
a.   Cedar County, Iowa, Deed Book W:4, Martin Marker & wife Margaret to George Galbraith, date of instrument 12 August 1865, date of filing 12 August 1865; Recorder's Office, Tipton.
b.   Cedar County, Iowa, Deed Book W:5, Martin Marker & wife Margaret to Alexander Moffett, date of instrument 12 August 1865, date of filing 12 August 1865; Recorder's Office, Tipton.
c.   Cedar County, Iowa, Deed Book W:6, Martin Marker & wife Margaret to Thomas & Frances Moffett, date of instrument 12 August 1865, date of filing 12 August 1865; Recorder's Office, Tipton.
d.   Cedar County, Iowa, Deed Book W:64, Martin Marker & wife Margaret to Martin V. Marker, date of instrument 12 August 1865, date of filing 26 October 1865; Recorder's Office, Tipton.
e.   Cedar County, Iowa, Deed Book W:276, Martin Marker & wife Margaret to William Moffett, date of instrument 12 September 1865, date of filing 5 June 1886; Recorder's Office, Tipton.
f.   Cedar County, Iowa, Deed Book W:138, Martin Marker & wife Margaret to Richard Jackson, date of instrument 25 October 1865, date of filing 23 January 1886; Recorder's Office, Tipton.
g.   Cedar County, Iowa, Deed Book W:79, Martin Marker & wife Margaret to George Boomershine, date of instrument 3 November 1865, date of filing 3 November 1865; Recorder's Office, Tipton.
h.   Cedar County, Iowa, Deed Book W:119, Martin Marker & wife Margaret to George & John Potter, date of instrument 1 January 1866, date of filing 1 January 1866; Recorder's Office, Tipton.
i.   Cedar County, Iowa, Deed Book Y:47-48, Martin Marker & wife Margaret to Conrad Miller, date of instrument 2 February 1866, date of filing 18 December 1866; Recorder's Office, Tipton.
j.   Cedar County, Iowa, Deed Book W:560, Martin Marker & wife Margaret to Christopher Stotler, date of instrument 17 February 1866, date of filing 19 January 1867; Recorder's Office, Tipton.
k.   Cedar County, Iowa, Deed Book 14:381, Martin Marker & wife Margaret to Baldwin Parsons, date of instrument 7 April 1866, date of filing 19 January 1867; Recorder's Office, Tipton.
l.   Cedar County, Iowa, Deed Book Y:117, Martin Marker & wife Margaret to Richard Jackson, date of instrument 18 September 1866, date of filing 18 January 1867; Recorder's Office, Tipton.
m.   Cedar County, Iowa, Deed Book W:403, Martin Marker & wife Margaret to Robert Maxwell, date of instrument 21 September 1866, date of filing 22 September 1866; Recorder's Office, Tipton.

103 Cedar County, Iowa, Deed Book W:3, William Derickson to Martin Marker, date of instrument 12 Aug. 1865, date of recording 12 Aug. 1865; Recorder's Office, Tipton.

104 See Table 1.

One of those sales was to his son Martin V. Marker who also moved from Darke County to Cedar County.[105]

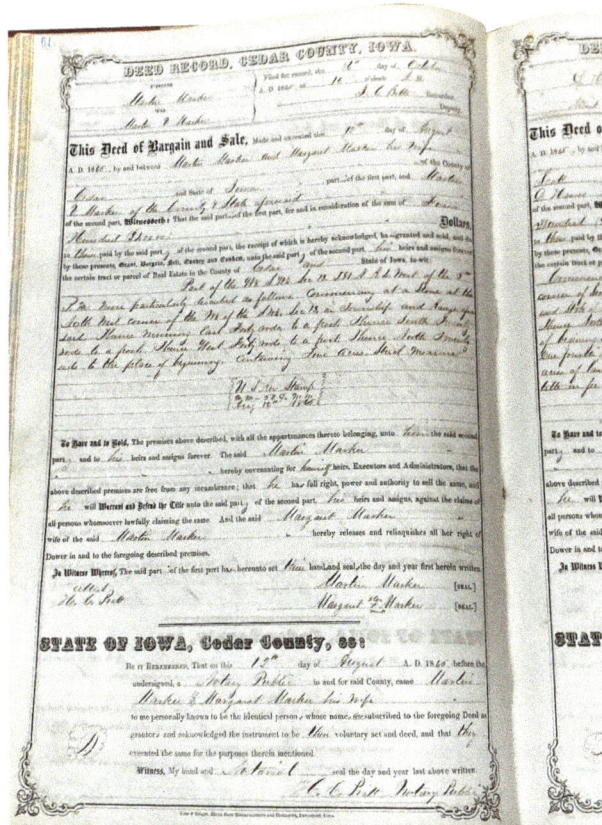

Cedar County, Iowa, Deed from Martin Marker to Martin V. Marker.

Early settlers to Iowa often purchased prairie land for farming and a smaller piece of timberland. "The woodland gave him logs for his house, fuel for his fires, and fences for his lots or fields; and the game of the woodland and the fish of the streams kept him in food."[106] The total sale price of the timberland lots was about $6,320, yielding a profit of about $1,120. An atlas of Cedar County from 1872 shows these small timberland lots created and sold by Martin Marker.[107]

---

105 Cedar County, Iowa, Deed Book W:64, Martin Marker & wife Margaret to Martin V. Marker, date of instrument 12 Aug. 1865, date of filing 26 Oct. 1865; Recorder's Office, Tipton.

106 Clarence Ray Auner, *Iowa Stories*, 4th ed. (Iowa City, Iowa: Clio Press, 1920), 1:47–48.

107 *Atlas of Cedar County Iowa* (Marshalltown, Iowa: Harrison & Warner, 1872), 47.

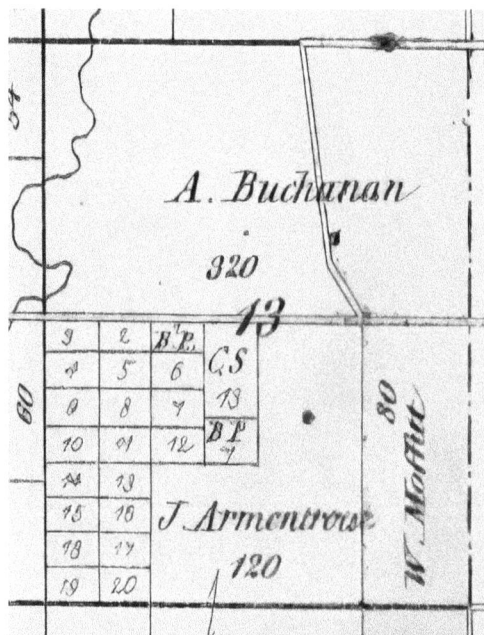

Martin Marker's Timberland Lots, from *Atlas of Cedar County
Iowa* (Marshalltown, Iowa: Harrison & Warner, 1872), 47; imaged
at Iowa Digital Library (digital.lib.uiowa.edu/islandora/object/
ui%3Aatlases_2892)

On 21 September 1866, Martin Marker sold his remaining land in Cedar County: a farm of 240 acres and 20 acres of timberland for $10,000.[108] He returned to Darke County because the purchaser of his Darke County farm failed to pay for it.[109]

Margaret (Weaver) Marker's father John Jacob Weaver died on 6 March 1868.[110] Margaret received three payments from his estate totaling $1,149.16 (including a $20 advance she received during her father's lifetime), worth about $25,000.00 today.[111] Margaret Marker and her husband, Martin, signed receipts for payments received. Martin signed his full name, but Margaret signed with an X, likely indicating she was

108 Cedar County, Iowa, Deed Book W:403, Martin Marker & his wife Margaret to Robert Maxwell, date of instrument 21 Sept. 1866, date of filing 22 Sept. 1866; Recorder's Office, Tipton.

109 *The History of Darke County, Ohio*, 612.

110 "Brief Mention of a Pioneer," *Dayton Daily Journal* (Dayton, Ohio), 17 March 1868, p. 1, col. 3. Ellerton Cemetery (Union Street, Montgomery Co., Ohio; LAT/LON 39.6798615, -84.3098243), John Jacob Weaver gravestone; read and photographed by author, 18 May 2022.

111 "Ohio, U.S., Wills and Probate Records, 1786–1998," database with images, Ancestry (www.ancestry.com) > Montgomery County > Probate Files, 9066-9086, 1850-1900 > images 361, 371 & 373 of 518, No. 9080, John Jacob Weaver, receipts dated 1 Oct. 1868, 1 Oct. 1869 & 1 Oct. 1870; citing Montgomery County Probate Court, Dayton. "Inflation Calculator," Official Data Foundation (www.in2013dollars.com).

unable to read or write.[112] Martin also received $5.00 from the estate for serving as the auctioneer when John Jacob Weaver's farm was sold.[113] Martin was "known as the best and most successful auctioneer in the county."[114]

Between 1860 and 1870, the population of Darke County increased from 26,009 to 32,278.[115] By 1870, Martin was back farming in Wayne Township, Darke County. His real estate was worth $11,000, and he owned $2,000 of personal property. He and Margaret had five children in their home: Manuel, age 24; Lucinda, age 15; Josiah, age 14; "Matilda," age 15; and Amanda, age 7.[116]

In Darke County in 1870, there were over 200,000 acres of cultivated land, which included 3,425 farms averaging 59.9 acres of improved land per farm. The most popular crops by number of acres farmed were corn, wheat, and oats.[117] Corn was always the most popular crop grown in Darke County, with twice as many acres devoted to corn than any other grain.[118]

The Marker family helped establish the Evangelical Trinity Lutheran Church, built in 1872, which was the first Lutheran Church in Versailles, Ohio.[119] Martin Marker contributed $100 towards the building of the church.[120] It was a large gift that was matched by only three others in the church.[121] Martin's brother Ezra donated $35, and his brother Perry donated $5.00.[122] Brother Lewis was also a member

---

112 "Ohio, U.S., Wills and Probate Records, 1786–1998," database with images, Ancestry, No. 9080, John Jacob Weaver receipts dated 1 Oct. 1868, 1 Oct. 1869 & 1 Oct. 1870.

113 "Ohio, U.S., Wills and Probate Records, 1786–1998," image 353, receipt dated 29 Aug. 1868.

114 *The History of Darke County, Ohio*, 612.

115 D. J. Lake & B. N. Griffing, *Atlas of Darke Co. Ohio* (Philadelphia: Lake, Griffing & Stevenson, 1875), 3.

116 1870 U.S. Census, Darke County, Ohio, pop. sched., Wayne Township, p. 378 (stamped), dwelling 1, family 1, Martin Marker household; imaged at Ancestry (www.ancestry.com); citing National Archives and Records Administration microfilm publication M593, roll 1194. The individualized agricultural schedule for Darke Co., Ohio, for 1870 did not survive. Form 82 Census Records—Research Ticket, National Archives and Records Administration, Service Ticket C11-763578097E, date searched 18 Aug. 22. What survived has aggregate numbers, not information about individual farmers. "1870: Agriculture, Darke County," National Archives and Records Administration (catalog.archives.gov/id/118679793).

117 Lake & Griffing, *Atlas of Darke Co. Ohio*, 12.

118 *The History of Darke County, Ohio*, 300.

119 Hilda Grace McPherson, comp., "Ohio Church Records, The Evangelica[l] Trinity Congregation now Trinity Lutheran Church Records, Versailles, Ohio, Darke, Wayne Township" (typescript, 1978, Fort Greenville Chapter, Daughters of the American Revolution; copy at Ohio State Library, Columbus), Intro.

120 McPherson, comp., "Ohio Church Records, The Evangelica[l] Trinity Congregation . . .," 6.

121 McPherson, comp., "Ohio Church Records, The Evangelica[l] Trinity Congregation . . .," 1.

122 McPherson, comp., "Ohio Church Records, The Evangelica[l] Trinity Congregation . . .," 2, 4.

of the church.[123] Margaret Marker is listed as the wife of a member.[124] Martin and Margaret's twin daughters, "Melinda" and Lucinda, were confirmed at the church on 26 March 1875.[125] On 26 September 1876, Martin was selected as a church elder for two years and his brother Perry was selected as an elder for one year.[126] On 3 June 1877, Martin was asked to continue as an elder until 1880.[127] Martin was a member of the Lutheran Church for over fifty years.[128] Some church records of the Evangelical Trinity Lutheran Church were kept in German; the church charter was written in German on one side of the book and English on the other.[129] The church is still operating today in a newer building as Trinity Lutheran Church.[130]

On 13 March 1879, Martin and Margaret's son Josiah married Isabella Lyons at the bride's parents' home in York Township in Darke County.[131] The wedding was a grand affair that made the local newspaper:

> Many friends were present at the wedding, [and] will long remember the day as being one of the bright ones in their lives. The feast was all that could have been desired by the most fastidious; the Dawn band being present, there was no lack of the most delightful music; and altogether it was one of the most enjoyable events of the season. The infare on the next day at Mr. M. Marker's was a decided success, no pains being spared by Mr. M. and his excellent lady to make the guests enjoy themselves.[132]

---

123 McPherson, comp., "Ohio Church Records, The Evangelica[l] Trinity Congregation . . .," 17.

124 McPherson, comp., "Ohio Church Records, The Evangelica[l] Trinity Congregation . . .," 18.

125 McPherson, comp., "Ohio Church Records, The Evangelica[l] Trinity Congregation . . .," 68.

126 McPherson, comp., "Ohio Church Records, The Evangelica[l] Trinity Congregation . . .," 51.

127 McPherson, comp., "Ohio Church Records, The Evangelica[l] Trinity Congregation . . .," 51.

128 "Death of an Old Pioneer," *Greenville Democrat*, 1 Nov. 1893.

129 McPherson, comp., "The Evangelica[l] Trinity Congregation," Intro.

130 McPherson, comp., "The Evangelica[l] Trinity Congregation," Intro. *Sesquicentennial Celebration, Versailles, Ohio*, 49. "Welcome to Trinity Lutheran Church," Trinity of Versailles (www.trinityofversailles .org/welcome).

131 "Ohio, U.S., County Marriage Records, 1774–1993," database with images, Ancestry (www.ancestry.com) > Darke County > 1878–1888 > image 74 of 581, p. 147, no. 439, Marker-Lyons, 13 March 1879; citing Darke County Courthouse, Greenville.

132 "Married," *Greenville Democrat* (Greenville, Ohio), 19 March 1879, p. 3, col. 2. An "infare" is a reception for a newly married couple. "Infare," Merriam-Webster (www.merriam-webster.com/dictionary/infare).

Isabella Lyons was the daughter of David Lyons and Mary Link.[133] David Lyons was one of the wealthiest settlers in York Township.[134]

By 1880, Martin and Margaret were in their sixties. Three single daughters lived with them: twins Lucinda and Malinda, age 25; and Amanda, age 17. A paid farmhand also lived with the family.[135] Martin farmed 140 tilled acres, had 5 acres that were permanent meadows, pastures, orchards, or vineyard, and had 24 acres of woodland. His farm was worth $12,000. He owned 3 horses, 4 milch cows, 5 other cattle, 9 swine, and 200 poultry. His livestock was worth $500. His farm produced 300 dozen eggs and 500 pounds of butter in the prior year.[136] Of the approximately 250 farmers in Wayne Township in Darke County, only two had farms worth more than his.[137]

Martin Marker was "one of the first farmers of the community, a first class sale crier [auctioneer], a veterinary, a clever citizen, and a prominent local politician . . . ."[138] "Old Mart" died on 24 October 1893 at the age of 78 of consumption in Versailles, Darke County, Ohio.[139] He lived long enough to see forty-eight grandchildren and seven great-grandchildren.[140] His widow, Margaret, died 24 January 1901 at age 83 of dropsy of the chest in Versailles.[141] They are buried together at Brock Cemetery.[142]

133 "Ohio Deaths, 1908–1953," database with images, FamilySearch (www.familysearch.org) > 1943 > 46901–49700 > image 3098 of 3321, no. 49503, Isabelle Marker, 23 Aug. 1943.

134 *The History of Darke County, Ohio*, 406.

135 1880 U.S. Census, Darke County, Ohio, pop. sched., Wayne Township, enumeration district 74, page 380 (stamped), dwelling 1, family 1, Martin Marker household; imaged at Ancestry (www.ancestry.com): accessed 7 Sept. 2022); citing National Archives and Records Administration microfilm publication T9, roll 1011.

136 1880 U.S. Census, Darke County, Ohio, agricultural schedule, enumeration district 74, p. 1, Martin Marker, imaged at Ancestry (www.ancestry.com); citing National Archives and Records Administration microfilm publication T1159, roll 59.

137 1880 U.S. Census, Darke County, Ohio, agricultural schedule, enumeration district 74, pps. 1–26.

138 Samuel Long, *A Pioneer History of Wayne Tp., Darke County, Ohio* ([pub. location unk.]: Radabaugh & Fahnestock, 1901), 44–45.

139 Long, *A Pioneer History of Wayne Tp.*, 44. Darke County, Ohio, death certificate, vol. 2, p. 154, Martin Marker, 24 October 1893; Probate Court, Greenville. Consumption is an old term meaning wasting of the body, particularly from pulmonary tuberculosis. "Medical Definition of Consumption," MedicineNet (www.medicinenet.com/consumption/definition.htm).

140 "Death of an Old Pioneer," *Greenville Democrat*, 1 Nov. 1893.

141 Darke County, Ohio, death certificate, vol. 2, p. 159, Margaret Marker, 24 Jan. 1901; Probate Court, Greenville. Dropsy is an old term meaning swelling from excess fluid. "Medical Definition of Dropsy," MedicineNet (www.medicinenet.com/dropsy/definition.htm).

142 Brock Cemetery (Darke Co., Ohio), Martin Marker & Margaret Marker gravestones.

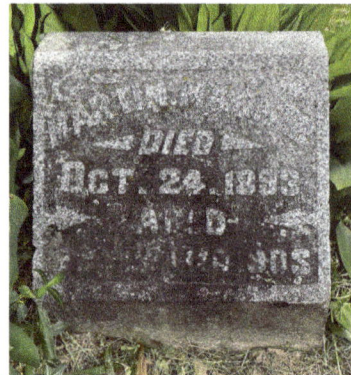

Martin and Margaret Marker gravestones at Brock Cemetery,
Darke County, Ohio.

Brock Cemetery is located on land that once belonged to Martin's brother Ezra. In 1847, Ezra Marker sold 1 acre of land in Section 4 of York Township in Darke County to the trustees of the Lutheran and German Reform congregation for $5.00.[143] That land became Brock Cemetery.[144] Also buried in Brock Cemetery is the famous

---

143 For land transaction: Darke County, Ohio, Deed Book R1: 138, Ezra Marker and wife Catharine to Samuel Windbeigher and Samuel Sherry as trustees for the Lutheran and German Reform, 27 Dec. 1847; Recorder's Office, Greenville. For brother relationship: Montgomery County, Ohio, Deed Record S:33, from Paul Marker to the children of George Marker, 14 March 1834; Montgomery County Archives, Dayton.

144 Darke County Visitors Bureau, *Official Map of Darke County, Ohio* (Map Works Inc., 2010). Anita Short and Ruth Bowers, *Cemetery Inscriptions Darke County Ohio*, 6 vols. (Greenville, Ohio: [pub. unk.], 1968), 2: 21.

sharpshooter Annie Oakley, a native of Darke County.[145] Interestingly, Ezra Marker is not buried there. He is buried at Greenlawn Cemetery in Greenville, Darke County.[146] Ezra's nephew Leonard Marker became one of the owners of Greenlawn Cemetery in 1896. Leonard was an undertaker and the son of Ezra's brother Raymond.[147]

Martin Marker died on 24 October 1893 without a will.[148] He reportedly gave his children $11,000 in lands and money during his lifetime, which may have accounted for the small size of his estate.[149] Some of his heirs expected that they would receive $400 apiece, but ultimately they received much less.[150]

Martin Marker's file in the Darke Probate Court lists as his heirs his wife, Margaret; his children Josiah Marker, Martha J. Murphy (wife of John Murphy), Lucinda Lehman (wife of Lawrence Lehman), Melinda Gulach (married to John Gulach), Amanda Shellenberger (married to Ellis Shellenberger), all of Darke County, Ohio; Martin V. Marker of Paton, Greene County, Iowa; Emanuel Marker of Greene County; Mary Wisener (married to Aaron Wisener) of Cedar County, Iowa; and his grandchildren James A. Lyons, Isaac Lyons, and Emanuel Lyons, all of Carroll County, Iowa.[151]

James, Isaac, and Emanuel Lyons were the sons of Lavina (Marker) Lyons. Lavina died in Carroll County on 16 May 1883 at age 45 after a lengthy illness.[152] Although Isaac and Emanuel were adults, their father, Jacob W. Lyons, was appointed their

145 Brock Cemetery (Greenville, St. Mary's Road, Darke County, Ohio; LAT/LON 40.2598818, -84.5609921), Annie Oakley gravestone; read and photographed by author, 17 May 2022.

146 Find a Grave, digital images (www.findagrave.com), memorial 138205047, Ezra Marker, photographs by "DJMonnier;" citing Greenlawn Cemetery, Versailles, Darke County, Ohio.

147 *A Biographical History of Darke County, Ohio: Compendium of National Biography*, 623.

148 Darke County, Ohio, Probate Court, Martin Marker Probate, Case No. 7146, microfilm roll #7; Probate Court Clerk's Office, Greenville.

149 *The History of Darke County, Ohio*, 612. A gift of land in Versailles, Ohio, from Martin Marker to his son Martin V. Marker was reported in the newspaper. "Register of Deeds," *Greenville Journal* (Greenville, Ohio), 4 June 1874, p. 3, col. 3.

150 Carroll County, Iowa, Probate Court File no. 714; In the Matter of the Guardianship of Isaac Lyons & Emanuel Lyons, Guardian Jacob Lyon's Petition for Discharge, 3 Feb. 1896; Probate Court Clerk's Office, Carroll.

151 Darke County, Ohio, Probate Court, Martin Marker Probate, Case No. 7146, microfilm roll #7; Probate Court Clerk's Office, Greenville.

152 "Death of Mrs. J. W. Lyons," *Carroll Herald* (Carroll, Iowa), 23 May 1883, p. 1, col. 5.

guardian for their share of their grandfather's estate because they were "imbeciles."[153] Isaac Lyons had whooping cough at the age of 2 and suffered from health problems for the rest of his life.[154] He was enumerated as "idiotic" in the 1880 census;[155] he died in 1919 from pneumonia at the age of 56.[156] Emanuel Lyons was institutionalized at the Iowa Hospital for the Insane at Clarinda for almost 29 years; he died there in 1918 at age 49 from tuberculosis.[157]

Son Josiah Marker served as the executor of his father Martin Marker's estate. The modest inventory of Martin's personal property was appraised at $73.80. The items included, among other things, a buggy, a wheelbarrow, an iron kettle, 1 hog's head, 10 bushels of corn, 6 bushels of oats, 1½ tons of hay, 2 bushels of clover seed, 3 forks, 6 chairs, and some household furniture. At the time of his death, Martin Marker owned three properties in Darke County:

- 50 acres in the SE quarter of Section 8, Township 10, Range 4 East appraised at $1,550

- 50 acres in the NE quarter of Section 8, Township 10, Range 4 East appraised at $1,450

- Lots 2 and 3 in Wood's Addition to the Town of Versailles appraised at $450[158].

Martin's widow, Margaret, waived her right to dower in the properties.[159]

---

153 Darke County, Ohio, Probate Court, Martin Marker Probate, Case No. 7146, microfilm roll #7; Probate Court Clerk's Office, Greenville. Carroll County, Iowa, Probate Court File no. 714; In the Matter of the Guardianship of Isaac Lyons & Emanuel Lyons, Letters of Guardians, 10 Jan. 1894, Probate Court Clerk's Office, Carroll.

154 "Isaac N. Lyons," *Carroll Times* (Carroll, Iowa), 10 April 1919, p. 6, col. 3.

155 1880 U.S. Census, Darke County, Ohio, pop. sched., Wayne Township, enumeration district 74, p. 381 (stamped), dwelling 31, family 31, Isaac M. Lyons in J. W. Lyons household; imaged at Ancestry (www.ancestry.com); citing National Archives and Records Administration microfilm publication T9, roll 1011. Instructions to enumerators for the 1880 U.S. Census did not define "idiotic." "Measuring America: The Decennial Censuses From 1790 to 2000," U.S. Census Bureau (www2.census.gov/library/publications/2002/dec/pol_02-ma.pdf), 19.

156 "Iowa Death Records, 1904–1951," database with images, FamilySearch (www.familysearch.org) > Film #102842708 > image 2639 of 5988, no. 14-01779, Isaac Newton Lyons, 7 April 1919.

157 "Iowa Death Records, 1904–1951," database with images, FamilySearch (www.familysearch.org) > Film # 102902986 > image 4290 of 16956, no. 73-2429, Emanuel R. Lyons, 21 March 1918.

158 Darke County, Ohio, Probate Court, Martin Marker Probate, Case No. 7146, microfilm roll #7; Probate Court Clerk's Office, Greenville.

159 Darke County, Ohio, Probate Court, Martin Marker Probate. Under Ohio law at the time, a widow or widower was "endowed of an estate for life in one-third of all the real property" owned by the spouse at the time of death. Ohio Rev. Stat. § 4188 (1890).

A public auction held on 24 March 1894 brought no bidders, so the land was sold through private sales. Son-in-law L. L. Lehman purchased the 100 acres in Section 8 for $2,000 and Martin's widow, Margaret Marker, purchased the lots in Versailles for $300.[160] The lack of bidders at the public auction may have been the result of the economic conditions at the time. In 1894, the United States was still in the midst of an economic depression following the Panic of 1893.[161] Banks failed as people sought to withdraw their deposits, businesses failed including railroads, and 20 percent of the population was unemployed.[162] Crop prices declined, farmers couldn't pay their debts, and foreclosures on farm mortgages occurred.[163] The U.S. economy didn't recover until 1897.[164]

Five months after Martin Marker died, a creditor came forward to make a claim against the estate. On 3 April 1894, James W. Goodall filed a claim in probate court for $1,000, plus $110 in interest, based on a promissory note signed by Martin and Margaret Marker on 14 November 1891 secured by the 100 acres of land in Section 8.[165] The promissory note provided that in exchange for $1,000, in two years Martin Marker agreed to repay James Goodall the $1,000 back plus 8 percent interest.[166] James Goodall was a farmer and a neighbor of Martin and Martha Marker.[167]

160 For son-in-law relationship and for purchases: Darke County, Ohio, Probate Court, Martin Marker Probate, Case No. 7146, microfilm roll #7; Probate Court Clerk's Office, Greenville.

161 David O. Whitten, "The Depression of 1893," Economic History Association (eh.net/encyclopedia/the-depression-of-1893/).

162 Sally Odekirk, "Living Through the Panic of 1893," FamilySearch (www.familysearch.org/en/blog/living-through-panic-of-1893).

163 Whitten, "The Depression of 1893."

164 Whitten, "The Depression of 1893."

165 Darke County, Ohio, Probate Court, Martin Marker Probate, Case No. 7146, microfilm roll #7; Probate Court Clerk's Office, Greenville.

166 Darke County, Ohio, Mortgage Book 64:402, Mortgage Deed from Martin Marker and wife, Margaret, to J. W. Goodall, date of instrument 14 Nov. 1891, date of recording 24 Nov. 1891; Recorder's Office, Greenville.

167 1880 U.S. Census, Darke County, Ohio, pop. sched., Wayne Township, enumeration district 74, p. 380 (stamped), dwelling 1, family 1, Martin Marker household; dwelling 3, family 3, James Goodall household; imaged at Ancestry (www.ancestry.com); citing National Archives and Records Administration microfilm publication T9, roll 1011.

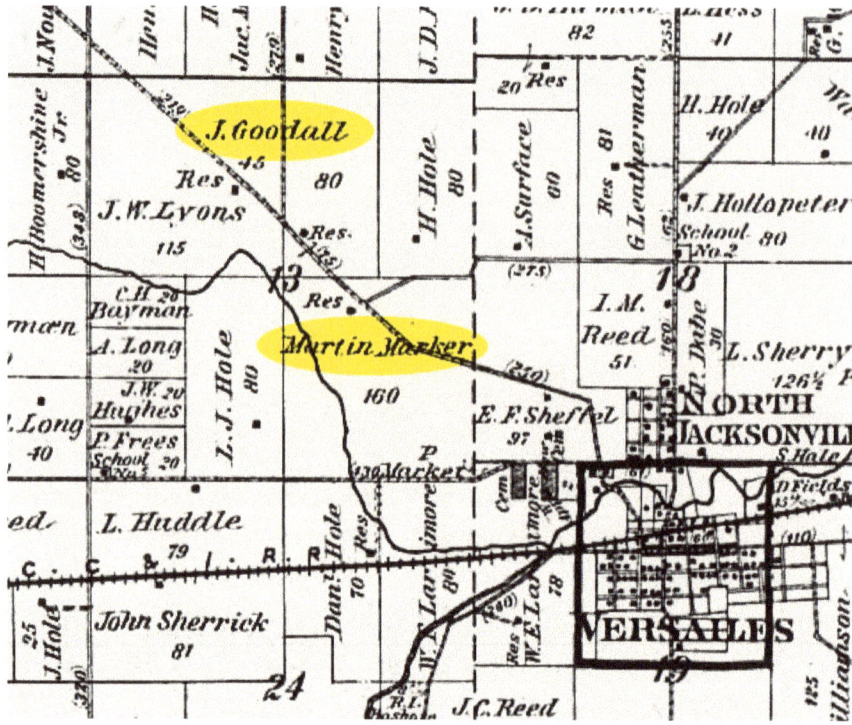

Darke County, Ohio, in 1875, from D. J. Lake & B. N. Griffing, *Atlas of Darke Co. Ohio* (Philadelphia: Lake, Griffing & Stephenson, 1875), 29; imaged at FamilySearch (www.familysearch.org).

At the time he took the loan from his neighbor, Martin was 76 years old and totally blind.[168] Although he usually signed legal documents with his full signature, he signed the promissory note with an X.[169]

---

168 "Death of an Old Pioneer," *Greenville Democrat*, 1 Nov. 1893.

169 Darke County, Ohio, Mortgage Book 64:402, Mortgage Deed from Martin Marker and wife, Margaret, to J. W. Goodall, date of instrument 14 Nov. 1891, date of recording 24 Nov. 1891; Recorder's Office, Greenville. The Clerk's copy of the deeds in Table 1 include a signature for Martin Marker, not an X.

Signatures on 1891 mortgage to J. W. Goodall.

The loan may have been the modern day equivalent of a reverse mortgage—a way to provide Martin with some cash in his old age. The probate court found the debt to Goodall to be valid, and he was paid $1,180 out of the estate.[170]

Under Ohio law, a widow was allowed to keep certain personal property such as a sewing machine, a family Bible, 1 cow, up to 12 sheep, clothing, and housewares up to certain dollar values.[171] Where the personal property was insufficient to provide for the widow, the appraisers determined an amount of money to pay her out of the estate.[172] The widow was also entitled to money for her support for one year.[173] Martin Marker's personal property was insufficient to provide for his widow Margaret. The

170 Darke County, Ohio, Probate Court, Martin Marker Probate, Case No. 7146, microfilm roll #7; Probate Court Clerk's Office, Greenville.

171 Ohio Rev. Stat. § 6038 (1890).

172 Ohio Rev. Stat. § 6041 (1890).

173 Ohio Rev. Stat. § 6040 (1890).

appraisers determined she should receive $250 for her support and $40 in lieu of a cow.[174] Margaret ultimately received a total of $533.69 from Martin's estate.

Four daughters of Martin Marker and the children of Lavina (Marker) Lyons received the following payments from his estate:

Martha Murphy $36.33
Melinda Gerlach $36.68
Lucinda Lehman $61.54
Mary Wisener $36.43
J. A. Lyons. $12.11
J. W. Lyons . . . . $24.22.
(Guardian for Emanuel & Isaac Lyons)

Ohio law provided that when a person died intestate, his real property and his personal property (less the personal property that went to his widow) should be divided among his children in equal portions.[175] Thus, the children of Lavina (Marker) Lyons (who was deceased) were entitled to receive her share of the estate.[176] The probate file does not explain why Lucinda (Marker) Lehman received more than her sisters, why youngest daughter Amanda Shellenberger did not receive a payment, or why the Marker brothers did not receive payments. Perhaps they received money and property during their father's lifetime.

Lyda Ellen Marker

Lyda Ellen Marker was likely a child of Martin and Margaret (Weaver) Marker. She is buried in Brock Cemetery between Cornelius Marker and William C. Marker.[177] Her gravestone reads: Lyda Ellen, Daughter of M. & M. Marker, Died Apr. 28, 1851, [unreadable] & 2 d's.[178]

---

174 Darke County, Ohio, Probate Court, Martin Marker Probate, Case No. 7146, microfilm roll #7; Probate Court Clerk's Office, Greenville.

175 Ohio Rev. Stat. §§ 4159, 4163 (1890).

176 Ohio Rev. Stat. § 4166 (1890).

177 Brock Cemetery (Greenville, St. Mary's Road, Darke Co., Ohio; LAT/LON 40.2598818, -84.5609921), Cornelius Marker, Lyda Ellen Marker, and William C. Marker gravestones; read and photographed by author, 17 May 2022.

178 A book of cemetery inscriptions from 1968 recorded her gravestone as reading age 3 weeks and 2 days, but the book incorrectly lists her year of death as 1854 and her name as Lydia. Short and Bowers, *Cemetery Inscriptions Darke County Ohio*, 2: 31.

Lyda Ellen Marker's gravestone in Brock Cemetery
in Darke County, Ohio.

The following evidence supports that Lyda Ellen Marker was the child of Martin Marker and Margaret (Weaver) Marker:

- Martin and Margaret Marker had two children who died in infancy.[179]

- Lyda Ellen Marker's and Cornelius Marker's gravestones are next to each other in Brock Cemetery and match in size, style, and font.[180]

- Both Cornelius's and Lyda Ellen's gravestones list their parents as M. & M. Marker.

179 "Death of an Old Pioneer," *Greenville Democrat*, 1 Nov. 1893.

180 Find a Grave, digital images (www.findagrave.com), memorial 138691860 for Cornelius Marker, memorial 31853887 for Lyda Marker, photographs of gravestones by "DSON1492;" citing Brock Cemetery, Darke County, Ohio.

- Cornelius Marker was enumerated as 2 years old, born in Ohio, living with his inferred parents, Martin and Margaret Marker, in the 1850 U.S. Census in Darke County, Ohio.[181]

- According to his gravestone, Cornelius Marker died 3 January 1851 at the age of 2 years, 5 months, and 9 days, yielding an approximate date of birth of 25 July 1848. (That is consistent with his enumerated age of 2 in the 1850 U.S. Census.)

- Lyda Ellen was not enumerated with the family in the 1850 U.S. Census and died by 28 April 1851. Census day in 1850 was 1 June 1850.[182] She was likely born after 1 June 1850 and sometime before 28 April 1851. Helping to narrow down her date of birth, Martha Jane Marker was born on 25 May 1851. There was time for Margaret Marker to have given birth to Lyda Ellen in the two years and ten months between about 25 July 1848, when Cornelius was born, and 25 May 1851, when daughter Martha Jane Marker was born.

Marker gravestones in Brock Cemetery in Darke County, Ohio.

181 1850 U.S. Census, Darke Co., Ohio, pop. sched. Wayne Township, p. 308 (stamped), dwell. 83, fam. 83, Cornelius Marker in Martin Marker household.

182 "1850 Overview," United States Census (www.census.gov/history/www/through_the_decades/overview/1850.html).

Children of Martin Marker and Margaret (Weaver) Marker:

i. **LAVINA S. MARKER,** b. 12 Feb. 1838 at Montgomery Co., Ohio; d. 16 May 1883 at Carroll Co., Iowa;[183] m. Jacob W. Lyons on 7 April 1859 at Darke Co., Ohio.[184]

+2 ii. **MARTIN VAN BUREN MARKER,** b. 27 June 1840 at Brock, Darke Co.; d. 8 July 1922 at Long Beach, Los Angeles Co., Calif.;[185] m. Martha Jane Hoover on 28 May 1863 at Darke Co.[186]

iii. **MARY MARKER,** b. 27 March 1843 in Versailles, Darke Co.; d. 2 March 1936 at Tipton, Cedar Co., Iowa;[187] m. Aaron Wisener on 4 June 1863 at Darke Co.[188]

---

183 For father: Darke County, Ohio, Probate Court, Martin Marker Probate, Case No. 7146, microfilm roll #7; Probate Court Clerk's Office, Greenville. For parentage and birthdate: *The History of Darke County, Ohio*, 612. For date and place of death: "Death of Mrs. J. W. Lyons," *Carroll Herald* (Carroll, Iowa), 23 May 1883, p. 1, col. 5. For birthdate and birthplace: "Death From Accident, J. W. Lyons," *Carroll Herald* (Carroll, Iowa), 14 March 1907, p. 1, col. 1. No entry was found in the Carroll County death register for Lyons for 1883 after a page-by-page search. "Iowa, U.S., Death Records, 1880–1904, 1921–1952," database with images, Ancestry (www.ancestry.com) > Registers > 1883 > Carroll County > images 81–83 of 703. The Carroll County Recorder does not have a death record for Lavina Lyons. Sarah Haberl, Carroll, Iowa ([email address for private use]), to Carolyn Ladd, email, 3 June 2022, "Uncertified Copy of Death Certificate," Marker Genealogy Folder; privately held by Ladd, carolynladd@comcast.net, P.O. Box 47254, Seattle, Washington 98146.

184 "Ohio, U.S., County Marriage Records, 1774–1993," database with images, Ancestry (www.ancestry.com) > Darke County > 1817–1866 > image 411 of 816, no. 1735, Lyons-Marker, 7 April 1859; citing Darke County Courthouse, Greenville, Ohio.

185 California Department of Public Health, death certificate no. 22-030921, Martin Van Buren Marker, 8 July 1922; Bureau of Vital Statistics, Sacramento. "Martin V. Marker," *Paton Portrait* (Paton, Iowa), 13 July 1922, p. 1, col. 5.

186 "Ohio, U.S., County Marriage Records, 1774–1993," database with images, Ancestry (www.ancestry.com) > Darke County > 1817–1866 > image 595 of 816, p. 281, no. 563, Marker-Hoover, 28 May, 1863; citing Darke County Courthouse, Greenville.

187 "Iowa, U.S., Death Records, 1880–1904, 1921–1952," database with images, Ancestry (www.ancestry.com) > Certificates > 1936 > Cedar County > image 3905 of 28642, no. 238, Mrs. Aaron Wisener, 2 March 1936; citing State Historical Society of Iowa, Des Moines. "Mrs. Wisener, 93, Tipton, is Taken to Rest," *Quad-City Times* (Davenport, Iowa), 3 March 1936, p. 7, col. 1.

188 "Ohio, U.S., County Marriage Records, 1774–1993," database with images, Ancestry (www.ancestry.com) > Darke County > 1817–1866 > image 597 of 816, p. 285, no. 507, Wisener-Marker, 4 June 1863; citing Darke County Courthouse, Greenville.

iv. **EMANUEL MARKER,** b. 12 Sept. 1845 at Versailles; d. 3 March 1920 at Jefferson Township, Greene County, Iowa;[189] m. Eliza Miller on 1 Nov. 1872 at Darke Co.[190]

v. **CORNELIUS MARKER,** b. abt. 25 July 1848, prob. at Darke Co.; d. 3 Jan. 1851, prob. at Darke Co.[191]

vi. **LYDA ELLEN MARKER,** b. prob. bet. June 1850 and Aug. 1851, prob. at Darke Co.; d. 28 April 1851, prob. at Darke Co.[192]

vii. **MARTHA JANE MARKER,** b. 25 May 1851 at Darke Co.; d. 22 Nov. 1942 at Allen Co., Ind.;[193] m. John Murphy on 4 March 1869 at Darke Co.[194]

189 "Iowa, Death Records, 1904–1951," database with images, FamilySearch (www.familysearch.org) > Death Certificates, Greene County > 1904–1920 > image 2094 of 3537, no. 37 1401, Emanuel Marker, 3 March 1920; citing State Historical Society of Iowa, Des Moines. "Emanuel Marker Dead," *Jefferson Bee* (Jefferson, Iowa), 10 March 1920, p. 1, col. 4.

190 "Ohio, U.S., County Marriage Records, 1774–1993," database with images, Ancestry (www.ancestry.com) > Darke County > 1866–1878 > image 260 of 555, no. 2085, Marker-Miller, 1 Nov. 1872; citing Darke County Courthouse, Greenville.

191 Brock Cemetery (Greenville, St. Mary's Road, Darke Co., Ohio; LAT/LON 40.2598818, -84.5609921), Cornelius Marker gravestone; read and photographed by author, 17 May 2022. For parentage: In the 1850 census, Cornelius Marker is enumerated as 2 years old, born in Ohio, and living with his inferred parents Martin and Margaret Marker in Darke County, Ohio. 1850 U.S. Census, Darke Co., Ohio, pop. sched., Wayne Township, p. 308, dwell. 83, fam. 83, Cornelius Marker in Martin Marker household. Birthdate calculated from gravestone: Cornelius, son of M. & M. Marker, died Jan. 3 1851, age 2 years, 5 months and 9 days. A 25 July date of birth is consistent with his enumerated age of 2 years in the 1850 census. Census day was June 1, 1850. "1850 Overview," United States Census (www.census.gov/history/www/through_the_decades /overview/1850.html). A book of cemetery inscriptions erroneously records that his age was 1 year, but the author reads the stone as saying 2 years. Short & Bowers, *Cemetery Inscriptions Darke County Ohio*, 2: 31.

192 Brock Cemetery (Greenville, St. Mary's Road, Darke Co., Ohio; LAT/LON 40.2598818, -84.5609921), Lyda Ellen Marker gravestone; read and photographed by the author, 17 May 2022.

193 "Indiana, U.S., Death Certificates, 1899–2011," database with images, Ancestry (www.ancestry.com) > 1942 > roll 12 > image 745 of 2507, no. 32242, Martha Jane Murphy, 22 Nov. 1942; citing Indiana Archives and Records Administration, Indianapolis. "Mrs. John Murphy," *Palladium-Item* (Richmond, Indiana), 24 Nov. 1942, p. 10, col. 6.

194 "Ohio, U.S., County Marriage Records, 1774–1993," database with images, Ancestry (www.ancestry.com) > Darke County > 1866–1878 > image 119 of 555, no. 530, Murphy-Marker, 4 March 1869; citing Darke County Courthouse, Greenville.

viii. **LUCINDA MARKER**, twin, b. 12 May 1855 at Versailles; d. 25 March 1937 at Versailles;[195] m. Lawrence Lehman on 8 Dec. 1887 at Darke Co.[196]

ix. **MALINDA MARKER**, twin, b. 12 May 1855 at Versailles; d. 17 March 1928 at Versailles;[197] m. John Gerlach on 27 Nov. 1881 at Darke Co.[198]

x. **JOSIAH MARKER,** b. 28 March 1858 at Darke Co.; d. 25 Oct. 1936 at Versailles;[199] m. Isabella Lyons on 13 March 1879 at Darke Co.[200]

xi. **AMANDA MARKER,** b. 9 Nov. 1862 at Versailles; d. 14 July 1945 at Darke County;[201] m. Rolland E. Shellenberger on 5 April 1883 at Darke County.[202]

195 "Ohio Deaths, 1908–1953," database with images, FamilySearch (www.familysearch.org) > 1937 > 14701–17700 > image 2906 of 3299, no. 17342, Lucinda Marker-Lehman, 25 March 1937; citing Ohio Department of Health, Columbus. "Banker's Widow is Dead at Versailles," *Daily Advocate* (Greenville, Ohio), 26 March 1937, p. 1, col. 3.

196 "Ohio, U.S., County Marriage Records, 1774–1993," database with images, Ancestry (www.ancestry.com) > Darke County > 1886–1899 > image 90 of 832, no. 530, Lehman-Marker, 8 Dec. 1887; citing Darke County Courthouse, Greenville.

197 "Ohio Deaths, 1908–1953," database with images, FamilySearch (www.familysearch.org) > 1928 > 12501–15800 > image 2879 of 3584, no. 15140, Malinda Gerlach, 17 March 1928; citing Ohio Department of Health, Columbus, Ohio. "Lifelong Resident of Versailles Dies," *Dayton Daily News* (Dayton, Ohio), 19 March 1928, p. 17, col. 2.

198 "Ohio, U.S., County Marriage Records, 1774–1993," database with images, Ancestry (www.ancestry.com) > Darke County > 1878–1888 > image 268 of 581, no. 1701, Gerlach-Marker, 27 Nov. 1881; citing Darke County Courthouse, Greenville.

199 "Ohio Deaths, 1908–1953," database with images, FamilySearch (www.familysearch.org) > 1936 > 61201–64200 > image 1233 of 3250, no. 62344, Josiah Marker, 25 Oct. 1936; citing Ohio Department of Health, Columbus, Ohio. "Deaths and Funerals," *Richmond Item* (Richmond, Ind.), 28 Oct. 1936, p. 3, col. 2.

200 "Ohio, U.S., County Marriage Records, 1774–1993," database with images, Ancestry (www.ancestry.com) > Darke County > 1878–1888 > image 74 of 581, no. 439, Marker-Lyons, 13 March 1879; citing Darke County Courthouse, Greenville. "Married," *Greenville Democrat*, 19 March 1879, p. 3, col. 2.

201 "Ohio Deaths, 1908–1953," database with images, FamilySearch (www.familysearch.org) > 1945 > 39001–42200 > image 2447 of 3569, no. 41176, Amanda M. "Shellenbarger," 14 July 1945; citing Ohio Department of Health, Columbus. "Amanda Shellenberger Rites 2 p.m. Tuesday," *Piqua Daily Call* (Piqua, Ohio), 16 July 1945, p. 5, col. 4.

202 "Ohio, U.S., County Marriage Records, 1774–1993," database with images, Ancestry (www.ancestry.com) > Darke County > 1878–1888 > image 367 of 581, no. 434, Shellenberger-Marker, 5 April 1883; citing Darke County Courthouse, Greenville.

Martin Van Buren Marker and Martha Jane Hoover

MARTIN VAN BUREN MARKER was born on 27 June 1840 at Brock, Darke County, Ohio; he died on 8 July 1922 at Long Beach, Los Angeles County, California.[203] He married **Martha Jane Hoover** on 28 May 1863 at Darke County.[204] They were married by Henry Burns, a Methodist Episcopal minister.[205] Martha was born on 25 May 1842 at New Madison, Darke County, and died on 27 January 1922 at Long Beach.[206] Martha J. Hoover was the child of Ann Curtis and David Hoover.[207]

---

203 California Department of Public Health, death certificate no. 22-030921, Martin Van Buren Marker, 8 July 1922; Bureau of Vital Statistics, Sacramento. "Martin V. Marker," *Paton Portrait*, 13 July 1922.

204 "Ohio, U.S., County Marriage Records, 1774–1993," database with images, Ancestry (www.ancestry.com) > Darke County > 1817–1866 > image 595 of 816, no. 563, Marker-Hoover, 28 May 1863; citing Darke County Courthouse, Greenville.

205 For name of officiant: "Ohio, U.S., County Marriage Records, 1774–1993," database with images. For officiant's denomination: *The History of Darke County, Ohio*, 405.

206 California Department of Public Health, death certificate no. 22-001890, Mrs. Martha J. Marker, 27 Jan. 1922; Bureau of Vital Statistics, Sacramento. "Death of Mrs. M. V. Marker," *Paton Portrait* (Paton, Iowa), 9 Feb. 1922, p. 2, col. 1.

207 California death cert. no. 22-001890, Mrs. Martha J. Marker, 27 Jan. 1922.

In 1863 when he was 22 years old, newly married, and living in Wayne Township of Darke County, Martin V. Marker registered for the draft for the Civil War.[208] There is no evidence that he served.[209] Over 300,000 Ohioans served during the Civil War, and more than 35,000 died.[210] One of them was Martin V. Marker's double first cousin Jacob Marker, son of Ezra Marker and Catharine (Weaver) Marker.[211] Jacob served as a private in Company E of the 47th Ohio Infantry. He died 12 August 1865 at the age of 21 in a hospital in Little Rock Arkansas of typhoid malarial fever.[212] Jacob is buried in the National Cemetery in Little Rock, Arkansas.[213]

208 "U.S., Civil War Draft Registration Records, 1863–1865," database with images, Ancestry (www.ancestry .com) > Ohio > 4th Congressional District > vol. 2 of 4, p. 327 > image 94 of 563.

209 Fold3 (www.Fold3.com), search for Martin Marker + Ohio + Civil War.

210 "Ohio in the Civil War: Interesting Facts," Ohio History Connection (www.ohiohistory.org/ohio-in-the-civil -war-interesting-facts/).

211 Obituary for Ezra Marker, newspaper unk., 1893; in the collection of the Garst Museum, Greenville, Ohio.

212 Carded medical record, Jacob Marker, Pvt. Co. E, 47th Ohio Regiment, Civil War; Carded Medical Records of Volunteer Soldiers in the Mexican and Civil Wars, 1846–1865; Record Group 94; Records of the Adjutant General's Office, 1762–1984; National Archives and Records Administration, Washington, D.C. "Official Roster of the Soldiers of the State of Ohio in the War of the Rebellion, 1861–1866," 12 vols. (Akron, Ohio: Werner Printing, 1887), IV:410.

213 "U.S., Civil War Roll of Honor, 1861–1865," database with images, Ancestry (www.ancestry.com) > vol. XXVI > National Cemetery, Little Rock, Arkansas > p. 172 > image 26 of 55, Jacob Marker. Find a Grave, digital image (www.findagrave.com), memorial 3138656 for Jacob Marker, photograph of gravestone by Whitney McLaughlin; citing Little Rock National Cemetery, Pulaski County, Ark.

Civil War carded medical record for Jacob Marker.

Martin V. Marker and his family moved from Darke County, Ohio, to Cedar County, Iowa, along with his father, Martin Marker.[214] Martin V. Marker first purchased land in Cedar County on April 21, 1864 when, for $1,500, he purchased 80 acres from Robert McClelland and his wife, Phebe, in Section 9 of Red Oak Township. The deed identifies Martin V. as being of the county of Cedar.[215] Martin V. Marker sold 20 acres of land in Darke County for $550 that was recorded on 30 April 1866.[216]

In 1870, the Martin V. Marker family lived in Red Oak Township in Cedar County where he worked as a farmer and Martha J. kept house. There were three children in the home: Emma J., age 3; Annie L., age 2; and Milburn M., age 1.[217] Red Oak was located about 6 miles north of Tipton, Iowa. It had prairie land with deep rich soil.[218]

As of 1870, M. V. Marker owned 80 acres of improved land in Red Oak and 10 acres of woodland—worth a total of $3,000. He had 3 horses, 2 milch cows, 1 cattle, and 5 swine—worth a total of $300. He grew spring wheat, corn, oats, potatoes, and hay; his cows produced $200 worth of butter in the previous year. The estimated total value of his farm production in the previous year was $1,010.[219]

The last property transaction in Cedar County involving Martin V. Marker and his wife, Martha J., was a $2,900 sale to Williamson Helmer that took place on 14 September 1871 and was for 80 acres in Section 7 of Red Oak Township and an additional 10 acres in Section 13.[220] An auction was announced in the local newspaper on 14 September 1871 for the sale of M. V. Marker's "milch cows, young cattle, Berkshire hogs, corn, hay, reaper, and other machinery and implements."[221] The family was moving west again, that time to Greene County, Iowa.

214 "Martin V. Marker," *Paton Portrait*, 13 July 1922.

215 Cedar County, Iowa, Deed Book T:477 Robert McClelland and his wife, Phebe Ann, to Martin V. Marker, date of instrument 21 April 1864, date of recording 25 Oct. 1865; Recorder's Office, Tipton.

216 "List of Transfers," *Greenville Journal*, 2 May 1866, p. 2, col. 3.

217 1870 U.S. Census, Cedar County, Iowa, pop. sched., Red Oak Township, p. 324 (*Greene County, Iowa* stamped), dwelling 49, family 49, M. V. Marker household; imaged at Ancestry (www.ancestry.com); citing National Archives and Records Administration microfilm publication M593, roll 380.

218 Linda Betsinger McCann, *Lost Cedar County, Vanished Towns of the Cedar Valley* (Des Moines, Iowa: Iowan Books, 2013), 93.

219 1870 U.S. Census, Cedar County, Iowa, agricultural schedule, pps. 3 and 4 (handwritten), M. V. Marker; imaged at Ancestry (www.ancestry.com); citing National Archives and Records Administration microfilm publication T1156, roll 7.

220 Cedar County, Iowa, Deed Book 7:118, Martin V. Marker and his wife, Martha J., to William Helmer, date of instrument 14 Sept. 1871, date of recording 27 May 1872; Recorder's Office, Tipton.

221 "Auction," *Tipton Advertiser* (Tipton, Iowa), 14 Sept. 1871, p. 4, col. 1.

AUCTION.— M. V. Marker, at his residence five miles south of Mechanicsville, sells on Friday, 22d inst., milch cows, young cattle, Berkshire hogs, corn, hay, reaper and other machinery and implements.

"Auction," *The Tipton Advertiser* (Tipton, Iowa),
14 September 1871, page 4, column 1

The first white settlers came to Greene County, Iowa, in 1849.[222] Swedes made up the largest ethnic group of white settlers of the county; the next largest group was Germans.[223] Corn was the most important crop in Iowa; the parts of the state with Clarion-Webster soil, including Greene County, are still particularly productive in growing corn.[224]

The town of Paton is located in the northeast corner of Greene County.[225] Paton Township, which contains the town of Paton, was settled later than other parts of the county because it was swampland that had to be drained by the laborious work of digging ditches and laying tile by hand.[226] In 1876, the town of Paton had a population of 84 people; by 1886 the population was 214.[227] Paton gets its name from a wealthy pioneer landholder from New York City named William Paton, who left a bequest to fund a public library that still exists today.[228]

Railroads played an important part in the settlement of Iowa. "No facet of the westward movement is more important than the story of the railroads, an assertion which has particular significance in Iowa history."[229] The first railroad to cross Iowa was completed in 1869; known as the Chicago & Northwestern Railway, it went east–west, and was built to link Chicago and Omaha. It had 24.52 miles of track

---

222 E. B. Stillman, *Past and Present of Greene County, Iowa* (1907; repr. Jefferson, Iowa: Greene County, Iowa, Genealogy Society, 1979), 24.

223 *Cavalcade of a Century* (Jefferson, Iowa: Greene Co. Centennial Committee, 1954), 29.

224 Leland L. Sage, *A History of Iowa* (Ames, Iowa: Iowa State University Press, 1974), 12–13.

225 Stillman, *Past and Present of Greene County*, Iowa, 184.

226 Wiltse McWilliam, "Northeast Greene County History," *Globe-Free Press* (Grand Junction, Iowa), 10 July 1969, p. 130, cols. 3–6.

227 McWilliam, "Northeast Greene County History."

228 For bequest: Stillman, *Past and Present of Greene County, Iowa*, 185. For library today: "William Paton Public Library," (www.paton.lib.ia.us).

229 Sage, *A History of Iowa*, 108–109.

in Greene County.[230] Another railroad—that one going south–north—started in Des Moines and went to Ft. Dodge; in 1869, it came through Greene County and through Paton.[231] Railroads allowed for the year-round transportation of people and products. Iowa farmers could ship their corn, wheat, beef, and pork to Chicago, and from there it could be shipped to the East Coast.[232] By 1883, there were 24 trains, both passenger and freight, going through the town of Paton every day.[233]

---

230 Stillman, *Past and Present of Greene County, Iowa*, 86.

231 Sage, *A History of Iowa*, 87.

232 Dorothy Schwieder, "History of Iowa," State Library of Iowa (publications.iowa.gov/135/1/history/7-1.html).

233 *Paton, the Heartland of Iowa, 1875–1975, 100 Years* (Paton, Iowa: [no pub.], 1975), 43; in the collection of the Greene County, Iowa, Historical Society.

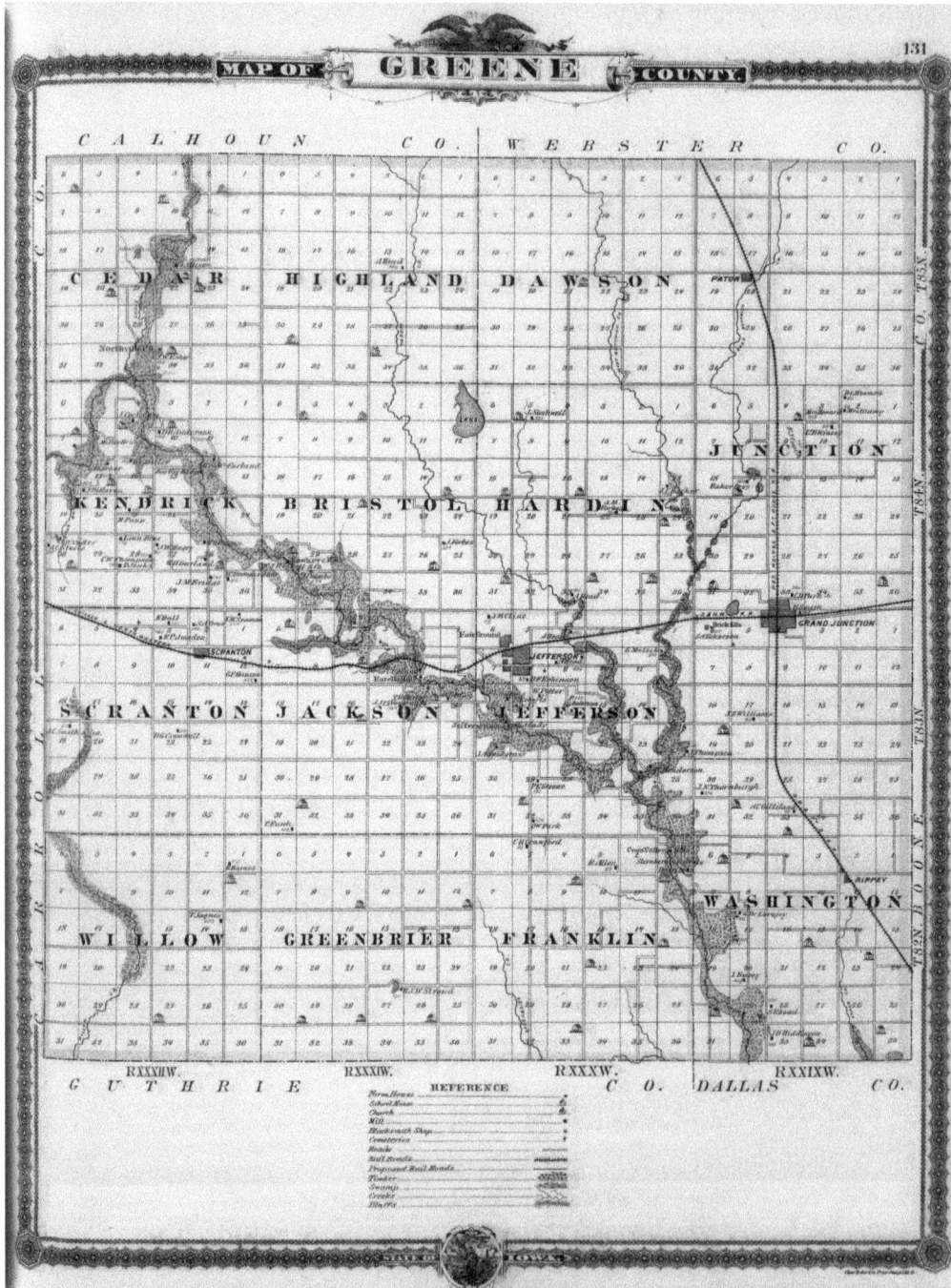

Greene County, Iowa, 1875, from A. T. Andreas, *Illustrated Historical Atlas of the State of Iowa* (Chicago: Andreas Atlas Co., 1875), 131; imaged at David Rumsey Map Collection (www.davidrumsey.com).

Martin V. Marker bought 104 acres of land in Section 18 of Paton Township in Greene County, Iowa, for $1,144 from Williamson Helmer and his wife, Matilda, of Cedar County, Iowa.[234] Williamson Helmer was a wealthy landowner and banker.[235] He was reputed to be one of the richest people in Cedar County; when he died in 1905, his estate was estimated at $150,000.[236] (Helmer also bought Martin V. Marker's property when he left Cedar County in 1871.)[237] On January 31, 1872, Martin V. Marker sued Helmer for failing to convey to him the land in Greene County per their written agreement.[238] Ten days after after the lawsuit was filed, Helmer and his wife signed the deed in front of a notary in Cedar County; it was filed in Greene County on 17 February 1872.[239] The litigation was settled on 13 February 1872 and resulted in Marker having a $310 lien for his litigation costs against Helmer, worth about $7,500 today.[240] Helmer paid the lien on 9 October 1874.[241]

Martin V. Marker was initially a farmer in Greene County, and then was a businessman in Paton for thirty years.[242] In 1880, the family lived in Paton Township where Martin V. Marker was a farmer, Martha was a homemaker, and they had seven children: Emma, age 14; Laura, age 13; Milburn, age 11; Cornelius, age 9; Mary, age 5; Jessie, age 3; and Harriet, age 5 months.[243] Martin Marker owned 70 tilled acres, 2

234 Greene County, Iowa, Deed Book O:169, Williamson Helmer and Matilda, his wife, to Martin V. Marker, date of instrument 10 Feb. 1872, date of filing 17 Feb. 1872; Recorder's Office, Jefferson.

235 "Pioneer Banker Dead, Williamson Helmer Passes Away at Mechanicsville," *Gazette* (Cedar Rapids, Iowa), 22 Feb. 1905, p. 10, col. 5.

236 "From All Over Iowa," *Evening Times-Republican* (Marshalltown, Iowa), 3 March 1905, p. 4, col. 5.

237 Cedar County, Iowa, Deed Book 7:118, Martin V. Marker and his wife, Martha J., to William Helmer, date of instrument 14 September 1871, date of recording 27 May 1872; Recorder's Office, Tipton.

238 "General Index, 1868–1886, Court Records, 1869–1886," digital images, FamilySearch (www.familysearch .org) > Film #008312025 > image 662 of 852, case no. 916, Marker v. Helmer; citing Cedar County Courthouse, Tipton.

239 Greene County, Iowa, Deed Book O:169, Williamson Helmer and Matilda, his wife, to Martin V. Marker, date of instrument 10 Feb. 1872, date of filing 17 Feb. 1872; Recorder's Office, Jefferson.

240 "General Index, 1868–1886, Court Records, 1869–1886," digital images, FamilySearch (www.familysearch .org) > Film # 008312007 > image 1257 of 1588, vol. 1, p. 427; citing Cedar County Courthouse, Tipton. "General Index to Liens, 1839–1900," digital images, FamilySearch (www.familysearch.org) > Film # 008584751 > image 331 of 616, no. 916, Judgment for Costs, in favor of Martin V. Marker, against Williamson Helmer; citing Cedar County Courthouse, Tipton. "Inflation Calculator," Official Data Foundation (www.in2013dollars.com).

241 "General Index to Liens, 1839–1900," no. 916, Judgment for Costs, in favor of Martin V. Marker against Williamson Helmer.

242 "Martin V. Marker," *Paton Portrait*, 13 July 1922.

243 1880 U.S. Census, Greene County, Iowa, pop. sched., Paton, enumeration district 88, p. 14 (handwritten), dwelling 87, family 90, Martin Marker household; imaged at Ancestry (www.ancestry.com); citing National Archives and Records Administration microfilm publication T9, roll 341.

acres of pastureland, and 153 acres of other improved land. The value of his farm was $3,375, and the value of his livestock was $400. That livestock included 3 horses, 2 milch cows, 84 swine, and 75 barnyard poultry.[244]

In 1885, Martin V. was still farming in Paton Township and there were seven children living in the home with him and Martha: Emma J., age 19; Milburn M., age 16; Cornelius C., age 14; Mary T., age 10; Jessie E., age 8; Harriet V., age 5; and John A., age 2.[245]

By 1900, Martin V. and Martha lived in the town of Paton with their three daughters: Mary, age 25; Jessie, age 23; and Harriet, age 20. Martin V. worked as a stock buyer; the family no longer lived on a farm and owned their home free of any mortgage.[246] In 1905, Martin V. was 65 years old, and he ran a creamery.[247] He and Martha lived in a home worth $3,000 with no mortgage.[248] Martin V. also bought and sold livestock, including the purchase and shipment of 15 coops of chickens, for which he paid the farmers $190.84.[249] On May 28, 1913, Martin V. and Martha J. celebrated their golden wedding anniversary; they went to nearby Gowrie, Iowa, to have their picture taken.[250]

244 1880 U.S. Census, Greene County, Iowa, agricultural schedule, pps. 14 and 15 (handwritten), Martin Marker; imaged at Ancestry (www.ancestry.com); citing National Archives and Records Administration microfilm publication T1156, roll 23.

245 "Iowa, U.S., State Census Collection, 1836–1925," database with images, Ancestry (www.ancestry.com) > 1885 > Greene > Paton > image 13 of 29, Martin V. Marker; citing State Historical Society of Iowa, Des Moines.

246 1900 U.S. Census, Greene County, Iowa, pop. sched., Paton, enumeration district 95, p. 150 (stamped), dwelling 52, family 52, Martin V. Marker household; imaged at Ancestry (www.ancestry.com); citing National Archives and Records Administration microfilm publication T623, roll 433.

247 "Iowa State Census, 1905," database with images, FamilySearch (www.familysearch.org) > image 1483 of 5193, M. V. Marker; citing Iowa Historical Society, Des Moines.

248 "Iowa State Census, 1905," database with images, FamilySearch (www.familysearch.org) > image 1250 of 5193, Martha J. Marker; citing Iowa Historical Society, Des Moines.

249 "Paton," *Paton Portrait* (Paton, Iowa), 16 Oct. 1908, p. 1, col. 1.

250 "Paton," *Grand Junction Globe* (Grand Junction, Iowa), 4 June 1913, p. 5, col. 6.

Martin V. and Martha J. Marker, 1913. From the collection of John R. Ladd.

As of 1915, at the age of 74, Martin V. was still in the cream business, working as a cream buyer; in 1914 he earned $300.[251] The Markers had their house wired for electricity in December 1915.[252] By 1920, Martin V. was 79 years old and retired, living in the town of Paton with his 77-year-old wife, Martha.[253]

251 "Iowa, U.S., State Census Collection, 1836–1925," database with images, Ancestry (www.ancestry.com) > 1915 > Greene > Paton > image 543 of 988, M. V. Marker; citing State Historical Society of Iowa, Des Moines.

252 "Local News," *Paton Portrait* (Paton, Iowa), 23 Dec. 1915, p. 1, col. 6.

253 1920 U.S. Census, Green County, Iowa, pop. sched., Paton, enumeration district 116, p. 138 (stamped), dwelling 62, family 67, Martin Marker household; imaged at Ancestry (www.ancestry.com); citing National Archives and Records Administration microfilm publication T625, roll 491.

Martin V. Marker's Siblings

Three of Martin V.'s siblings moved to Greene County, Iowa: Josiah Marker, Emanuel Marker, and Lavina (Marker) Lyons. As of 1880, the three Marker brothers lived in neighboring townships and all were farmers: Martin lived in Paton, Josiah in Dawson, and Emanuel in Hardin.[254]

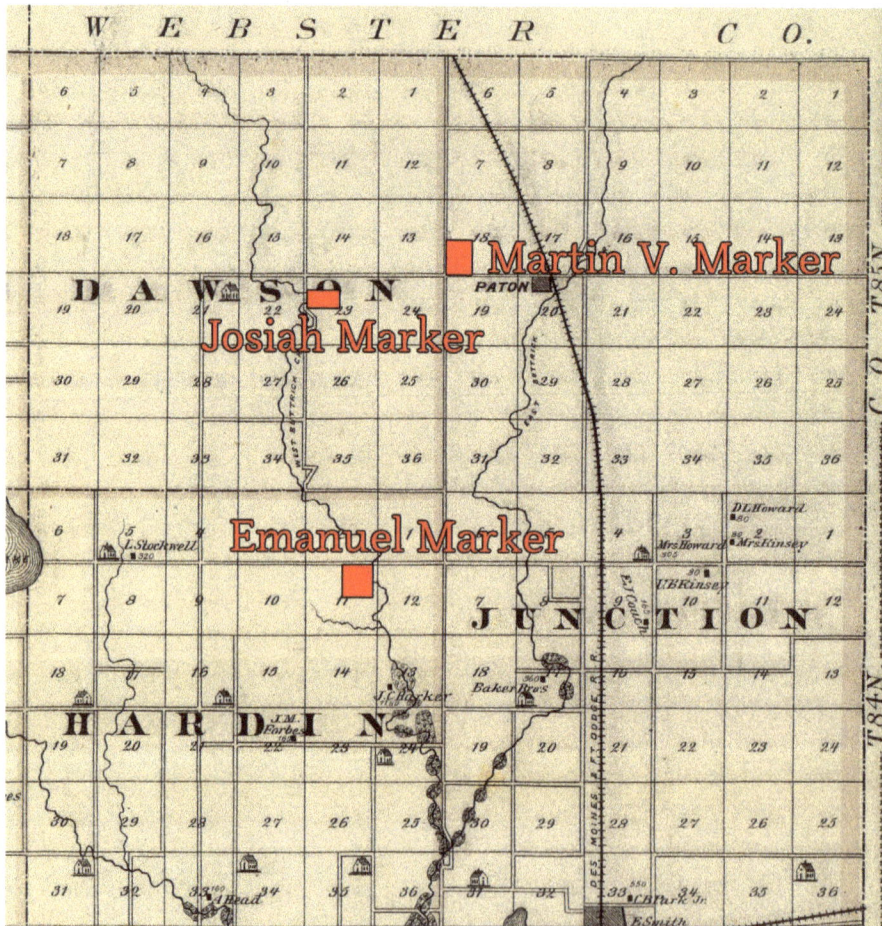

Marker Brothers' Land Purchases, from *Map of Greene County, State of Iowa* (Chicago: Andreas Atlas Co., 1875), 131; imaged at David Rumsey Map Collection (www.davidrumsey.com).

254 1880 U.S. Census, Greene County, Iowa, pop. sched., Paton Township, ED 88, p. 14, dwell. 87, fam. 90, Martin Marker household; Dawson Township, enumeration district 88, [handwritten p. no. illegible], dwelling 61, family 65, Josiah Marker household; Hardin Township, enumeration district 91, p. 8 (handwritten), dwelling 56, family 57, Emanuel Marker household; imaged at Ancestry (www.ancestry.com); citing National Archives and Records Administration microfilm publication T9, roll 341.

Josiah Marker

Josiah Marker first bought land in Greene County, Iowa, on 9 July 1879, in Dawson Township.[255] As of 1880, he farmed 70 acres of tilled land, and his farmland was worth $1,040. His livestock was worth $300 and included 2 milch cows, 10 swine, 2 horses, and 10 barnyard poultry.[256] In 1885, he was still farming in Dawson Township.[257]

Josiah and his wife, Isabelle, were Quakers.[258] In 1887, Josiah donated 1¼ acres of Section 15 of Dawson Township to the Paton Monthly Meeting of Friends "provided that said Paton Monthly Meeting of Friends builds a Church building on said land during the years 1887 and 1888." On 19 February 1891, a local Greene County newspaper announced that Josiah had rented his farm and was leaving Iowa to return to Ohio.[259] An advertisement announced a large public sale that included his farm equipment and livestock, including hogs, cattle, and horses.[260] He and his wife sold their farm in Greene County on 26 February 1892 to Uransey Weant, another member of the Society of Friends.[261] The sale to Uransey was for 158¾ acres of Section 15, excepting the 1¼ acres of land previously donated to the Paton Monthly Meeting of Friends for their church. The Quaker meeting house was, indeed, built on the land that Josiah had donated; it can be seen on a plat map of Greene County dated 1896.[262]

255 Greene County, Iowa, Deed Book Y:279, Malon Head to Josiah Marker, date of instrument 9 July 1879, date of filing 30 July 1879; Recorder's Office, Jefferson. Greene County, Iowa, Deed Book 27:6 James Callaman & his wife, Martha, to Josiah Marker, date of instrument 9 July 1879, date of filing 30 July 1879; Recorder's Office, Jefferson.

256 1880 U.S. Census, Greene County, Iowa, agricultural schedule, p. 20 (handwritten), "Joseph" Marker; imaged at Ancestry (www.ancestry.com); citing National Archives and Records Administration microfilm publication T1156, roll 23.

257 "Iowa, U.S., State Census Collection, 1836–1925," database with images, Ancestry (www.ancestry.com) > 1885 > Greene > Dawson > image 12 of 21, Josiah Marker; citing State Historical Society of Iowa, Des Moines.

258 "U.S., Hinshaw Index to Selected Quaker Records, 1680–1940," database with images, Ancestry (www .ancestry.com) > Iowa > Paton Monthly Meeting > images 501, 502, and 503 of 897.

259 "Pertinent Points," *Jefferson Bee* (Jefferson, Iowa), 19 Feb. 1891, p. 1, col. 1.

260 "Public Sale," *Jefferson Bee* (Jefferson, Iowa), 19 Feb. 1891, p. 1, col. 6.

261 Greene County, Iowa, Deed Book 39:625, Josiah Marker and his wife, Isabell, to Uransey F. Weant, date of instrument 26 Feb. 1892, date of recording 3 March 1892; Recorder's Office, Jefferson. "Iowa State Census, 1915," database with images, FamilySearch (www.familysearch.org) > Greene > Vroman, R.–Zwicky > image 235 of 1432, U. F. Weant. "U.S., Hinshaw Index to Selected Quaker Records, 1680–1940," database with images, Ancestry (www.ancestry.com) > Iowa > Paton Monthly Meeting > image 781 of 897.

262 *Plat Book of Greene County, Iowa*, (Philadelphia: F. Bourquin, 1896), 5; imaged at Iowa Digital Library (digital.lib.uiowa.edu/islandora/object/ui%3Aatlases_6029). The location of the Paton Quaker meeting is listed as "Dawson Twp., Sec. 15, Twp. 85N, Rge. 30W." "Monthly Meetings in North America: A Quaker Index," QuakerMeetings.com (www.quakermeetings.com).

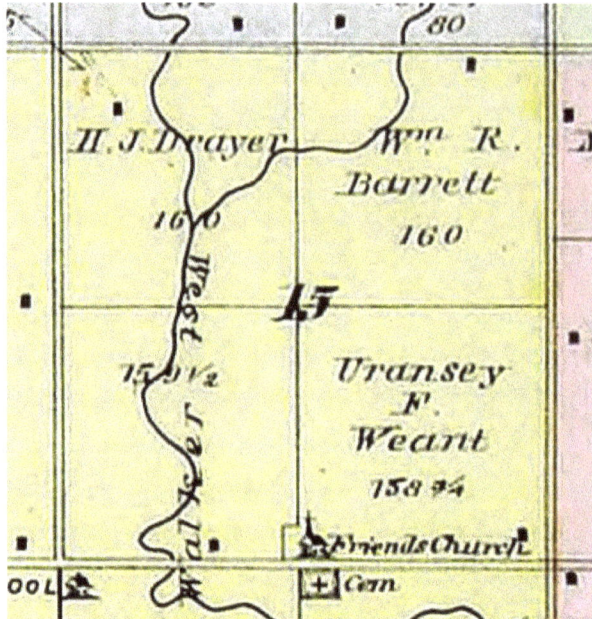

Friends meeting house on land donated by Josiah Marker, from
Plat Book of Greene County, Iowa (Philadelphia: F. Bourquin, 1896), 5;
imaged at Iowa Digital Library (digital.lib.uiowa.edu).

By 1892, Josiah and Isabelle were back in Darke County, Ohio.[263] Josiah may
have returned there to help his elderly father, Martin, who at that point was totally
blind.[264] After his father's death in 1893, Josiah served as the executor of the estate.[265]
Josiah remained in Darke County and died there 25 October 1936 at age 78.[266] He is
buried in Greenlawn Cemetery with his wife, Isabelle.[267]

---

263 Greene County, Iowa, Deed Book 39:625 Josiah Marker and his wife, Isabell, to Uransey F. Weant, date of
instrument 26 Feb. 1892, date of recording 3 March 1892; Recorder's Office, Jefferson.

264 "Death of an Old Pioneer," *Greenville Democrat*, 1 Nov. 1893.

265 Darke County, Ohio, Probate Court, Martin Marker Probate, Case No. 7146, microfilm roll #7; Probate
Court Clerk's Office, Greenville.

266 "Ohio Deaths, 1908–1953," database with images, FamilySearch (www.familysearch.org) > 1936 > 61201–
64200 > image 1233 of 3250, no. 62344, Josiah Marker, 25 Oct. 1936; citing Ohio Department of Health,
Columbus, Ohio. "Josiah Marker is Paralysis Victim, Retired Farmer Dies at Versailles; Rites Thursday," *Daily
Advocate* (Greenville, Ohio), 26 Oct. 1936, p. 1, col. 2.

267 Find a Grave, digital images (www.findagrave.com), memorial 141763653 for Josiah Marker, memorial
141763593 for Isabelle Marker, photographs by "DJMonnier;" citing Greenlawn Cemetery, Darke County,
Ohio.

Emanuel Marker

In 1878, Emanuel Marker bought 160 acres of land in Hardin Township, Greene County;[268] as of 1880, he farmed 136 tilled acres and had 25 unimproved acres there. His farmland was worth $3,400; his livestock was worth $500 and included 2 milch cows, 38 swine, 100 barnyard poultry, and 4 horses.[269] By 1900, he had 280 acres in Hardin Township and had 27 cattle, 43 hogs, 300 poultry, and 9 horses. He was considered one of the "well-to-do farmers of Greene County."[270] Emanuel and his brother Martin V. maintained a relationship over the years, and their visits were sometimes reported in the local paper.[271] Emanuel remained in Greene County for the rest of his life.[272] He died 3 March 1920 at age 74, and is buried with his wife, Eliza, in Jefferson Cemetery.[273]

Lavina (Marker) Lyons

Martin V. Marker's sister Lavina (Marker) Lyons and her husband, J. W. Lyons, moved to Greene County, Iowa, in 1882. They remained about a year and did not purchase any real property in Greene County.[274] They moved to neighboring Carroll County in 1882, where J. W. purchased a 120-acre farm for $3,700.[275] Lavina died in 1883 at

---

268 Greene County, Iowa, Deed Book 26:26 Albert Cosgriff to Emanuel Marker, date of instrument 23 May 1878, date of filing 24 May 1878; Recorder's Office, Jefferson. Greene County, Iowa, Deed Book 26:47, Greene County to Emanuel Marker, date of instrument 4 June 1878, date of filing 4 June 1878; Recorder's Office, Jefferson. Greene County, Iowa, Deed Book 26:53, John Cosgriff by the sheriff to Emanuel Marker, date of instrument 5 June 1878, date of filing 5 June 1878; Recorder's Office, Jefferson.

269 1880 U.S. Census, Greene County, Iowa, agricultural schedule, p. 6 (handwritten), Emanuel Marker; imaged at Ancestry (www.ancestry.com); citing National Archives and Records Administration microfilm publication T1156, roll 23.

270 The Stillman Brothers, eds., *The Greene County Book 1900, Statistics and Biography* (Jefferson, Iowa: *Jefferson Bee*, 1900), [no p. no.].

271 For example: "Paton," *Jefferson Bee* (Jefferson, Iowa), 4 Aug. 1915, p. 3, col. 4. "Paton," *Jefferson Bee* (Jefferson, Iowa), 17 July 1918, p. 6, col. 4.

272 "Emanuel Marker Dead," *Jefferson Bee* (Jefferson, Iowa), 10 March 1920, p. 1, col. 4.

273 *Biographical and Historical Record of Greene and Carroll Counties, Iowa* (Chicago: Lewis Publishing Co., 1887), 339. Jefferson Cemetery (East Lincoln Way, Greene Co., Iowa; LAT/LON 42.0146889, -94.3592106), Emanuel and Eliza Marker gravestones; read and photographed by author, 7 June 2022.

274 Greene County, Iowa, General Index Deeds, vols. 8, 9; Recorder's Office, Jefferson. There are no listings in the index from July 1879 to March 1886 for Lyons. "Death from Accident," *Herald* (Carroll, Iowa), 14 March 1907, p. 1, col. 1. J. W. Lyons died on 8 March 1907, the day after being crushed by a horse in a barn on his farm.

275 "Carroll County (Iowa) Deeds, 1855–1916," digital images, FamilySearch (www.familysearch.org) > Film #0085923 > image 280 of 1322, Deed Book U:551; citing Carroll County Courthouse, Carroll, Iowa. "Local Events of Interest," *Carroll Herald* (Carroll, Iowa), 6 Sept. 1882, page 4, col. 5.

age 45 from a long and painful illness that rendered her an invalid for the last fifteen years of her life.[276]

Other Siblings

Although they lived far apart, local newspapers reported visits to Paton, Iowa, by four of Martin V. Marker's sisters. Mary (Marker) Wisener visited her brothers M. V. and Emanuel in Paton in 1897; she had not seen them in twenty years.[277] Amanda (Marker) Shellenberger of Ohio visited her brother M. V. in 1909; she had not seen him in thirty years.[278] Lucinda (Marker) Lehman visited her brother M. V. in Paton in 1910; she had not seen him in twenty-eight years.[279] Martha Jane (Marker) Murphy of Ohio visited her brother M. V. in 1919.[280]

Religion

Martha (Hoover) Marker was confirmed in the Lutheran Church, but later joined the Methodist Episcopal Church.[281] The Methodist Church was founded in Paton in 1876;[282] the first Methodist Church building was completed in 1882.[283] Martha Marker and daughters Mary, Jessie, and Harriet were members of the Paton United Methodist Church.[284] In the 1895 Iowa census, Martin V., Martha, Mary, and Jessie Marker were identified as Methodist Episcopal.[285]

---

276 "Death of Mrs. J. W. Lyons," *Carroll Herald* (Carroll, Iowa), 23 May 1883, p. 1, col. 5.

277 "Local and Personal," *Paton Promoter* (Paton, Iowa), 7 Aug. 1897, p. 7, col. 4.

278 "The News in Greene," *Jefferson Bee* (Jefferson, Iowa), 25 Aug. 1909, p. 8, col. 5.

279 "Paton News Letter," *Jefferson Bee* (Jefferson, Iowa), 7 Sept. 1910, p. 8, col. 4.

280 "Personal Items," *Paton Portrait* (Paton, Iowa), 24 July 1919, p. 1, col. 5.

281 "Martha J. Hoover," *Paton Portrait* (Paton, Iowa), 3 Aug. 1922, p. 1, col. 6.

282 *Biographical and Historical Record of Greene and Carroll Counties, Iowa* (Chicago: Lewis Publishing Co., 1887), 523.

283 McWilliam, "Northeast Greene County History," *Globe-Free Press*, 10 July 1969.

284 "Paton-Salem United Methodist Church," Iowa State Archives microfilm 1738301, [no p. or slide no.], Record of Members in Full Connection; Des Moines, Iowa.

285 "Iowa State Census, 1895," database with images, FamilySearch (www.familysearch.org) > Greene > image 488 of 625, Martin, Martha, Mary, and Jesse Marker; citing State Historical Society of Iowa, Des Moines.

Paton United Methodist Church. Photo courtesy of the
Greene County Iowa Historical Society, Jefferson, Iowa.

The people of Iowa tried several times to outlaw the sale of liquor.[286] Martin V. and Martha Marker and their daughter Jessie Marker signed a Women's Christian Temperance Union petition in 1895, opposing a saloon being placed in Paton, Iowa, because of "the suffering brought upon innocent women and children from drink . . . ."[287] Their opposition to alcohol may have stemmed from their religious beliefs, as Methodists generally opposed alcohol.[288]

Martha Marker's church affiliation was enumerated in the 1915 Iowa census as Methodist Episcopal.[289] Martha Marker was an active member of the Methodist Episcopal Church of Paton for forty years.[290] Martin V. was enumerated in 1915 as having no church affiliation.[291] His obituary says that he was confirmed a Lutheran at the age of 14.[292]

286 Stillman, *Past and Present of Greene County, Iowa*, 19. "Early Temperance Activity in Iowa," *Iowa Pathways* (www.iowapbs.org/iowapathways/mypath/2631/early-temperance-activity-iowa).

287 "The News in Greene," *Jefferson Bee* (Jefferson, Iowa), 21 March 1895, p. 8, col. 4.

288 "Early Temperance Activity in Iowa," *Iowa Pathways.*

289 "Iowa, U.S., State Census Collection, 1836–1925," database with images, Ancestry (www.ancestry.com) > 1915 > Greene > Paton > image 542 of 988, M. J. Marker; citing State Historical Society of Iowa, Des Moines.

290 "Mrs. Martha J. Marker," *Long Beach Press* (Long Beach, Calif.), 27 Jan. 1922, p. 8, col. 4.

291 Iowa, U.S., State Census Collection, 1836–1925," database with images, Ancestry (www.ancestry.com) > 1915 > Greene > Paton > image 543 of 988, M. V. Marker; citing State Historical Society of Iowa, Des Moines.

292 "Martin V. Marker," *Patron Portrait* (Paton, Iowa), 3 Aug. 1922, p. 1, cols. 6–7.

TEACHER'S DAILY REGISTER.--FOR THE TERM

Winter Term

	MONTHS OF		November		December						
Number.	NAMES OF PUPILS.	Age.									Number Belonging
1	Leonard Mary	9									
2	" Charles	13									
3	Conant May	13									
4	" Clyde	9									
5	" Kate	7									
6	" Matthew	18									
7	Sargent John	13									
8	" Agnes	9									
9	" Bernard	19									
10	Avey Myrtie	12									
11	Roberts Lizzy	13									
12	Bright Lelia	13									
13	Sargent Stephen	15									
14	Russell Willie	14									
15	Roberts John	11									
16	" Cora	10									
17	Ferrell Frank	13									
18	Bright Martha	18									
19	Ferrell Edward	10									
20	Sargent Thomas	20									
21	Thomas James	6									
22	Avey Clara	5									
23	Number Belonging =										

Milburn Marker's Teacher's Daily Register, 1894.

COMMENCING *Nov. 13* 18*93*, AND ENDING *March 2,* 18*94.*

Milburn Marker Teacher

BRANCHES STUDIED

"Greene County, Iowa Teacher's Registers 1884–1900," digital images, *FamilySearch* (www.familysearch.org) > Film # 007733684 > Bristol, Farlin > image 803 of 844; citing the Greene County Courthouse, Jefferson, Iowa.

A Family of Teachers

Martin V. Marker's "great ambition was the education of his family."[293] As a young single woman, his future wife, Martha J. Hoover, had been a teacher in Ohio.[294] Education of their children was likely a high priority for her as well. Five of their children became teachers: Emma, Milburn, Mary, Jessie, and Harriet.

Between 1856 and 1900, Iowa built over 12,000 rural schools to educate farm children. Most of those were one-room schoolhouses. Schools were situated with the goal that no student would have to walk more than 2 miles to get to school.[295] A teacher's responsibilities at a one-room schoolhouse started with getting a fire going in the wood-burning stove in the morning, teaching a wide range of ages of children throughout the day, maintaining strict discipline, and ended with sweeping the floor at the end of the day.[296] Teaching methods involved memorization and recitation.[297] Iowa's free public education system was a success: by 1915, Iowa had the highest literacy rate in the country with 97.9 percent of adults able to read and write.[298]

Emma Marker worked as a teacher when she was 19 years old, single, and living with her parents in Paton.[299] Milburn Marker was also a teacher; for the 1893–1894 winter session, Milburn taught twenty-one students, ranging in age from 6 to 20, at Bristol #5 School in Farlin, Iowa. He taught them a number of subjects, including reading, grammar, arithmetic, geography, history, physiology, penmanship, and bookkeeping.[300]

---

293 "Martin V. Marker," *Patron Portrait* (Paton, Iowa), 3 Aug. 1922, p. 1, cols. 6–7.

294 1860 U.S. Census, Darke County, Ohio, pop. sched., Wayne Township, p. 273 (handwritten), dwelling 1923, family 1928, Martha J. Hoover; imaged at Ancestry (www.ancestry.com); citing National Archives and Records Administration microfilm publication M653, roll 956.

295 Sandra Kessler Host, *A New Look at Iowa's One-Room Schools: Iowa's Lost Treasure—A System of 12,623 Rural Schools 1858–1966* (Odebolt, Iowa: Rural Legacy Project, 2015), Intro, and p. 1; imaged at Iowa Rural Schools Museum (www.iowaruralschoolsmuseum.net).

296 "A Walk Through Iowa's One-Room Schoolhouses," Iowa Department of Education (educateiowa.gov/walk -through-iowa-s-one-room-schoolhouses).

297 Host, *A New Look at Iowa's One-Room Schools*, 19–20.

298 Host, *A New Look at Iowa's One-Room Schools*, 36.

299 "Iowa, U.S., State Census Collection, 1836–1925," database with images, Ancestry (www.ancestry.com) > 1885 > Greene > Paton > image 13 of 29, Emma Marker; citing State Historical Society of Iowa, Des Moines.

300 "Greene County, Iowa Teacher's Registers 1884–1900," digital images, FamilySearch (www.familysearch .org) > Film # 007733684 > Bristol, Farlin > image 803 of 844; citing the Greene County Courthouse, Jefferson, Iowa.

The first schoolhouse in Paton was constructed in 1886.[301] There were thirty-five students. Prior to that, school was held in a variety of locations, including an attic and a boxcar.[302] Three daughters of Martin V. and Martha graduated from Paton School: Mary graduated valedictorian in the first graduating class in 1889; Jessie graduated in 1892; and Harriet graduated in 1896.[303]

As of 1900, Mary, Jessie, and Harriet lived with their parents and all three worked as schoolteachers.[304] Mary (Marker) Griffith taught for sixty years until she retired in Timnath, Colorado, at the age of 76.[305] Jessie became the assistant supervisor of music in the Los Angeles city schools and worked there until her retirement.[306] Harriet worked as a teacher in the Paton schools and in rural schools for eight years before she married in 1905.[307] (At that time Iowa did not allow women to continue to teach after getting married.[308])

---

301 McWilliam, "Northeast Greene County History," *Globe-Free Press*, 10 July 1969.

302 *Cavalcade of a Century* (Jefferson, Iowa: Greene County Centennial Committee, 1954), 39; imaged at Internet Archive (archive.org).

303 "Graduates of the Paton High School," *Paton Portrait* (Paton, Iowa), 21 June 1928, p. 2, cols. 3–5. For valedictorian: "Mrs. Griffith, Former Timnath Teacher, Dies," *Fort Collins Coloradoan* (Fort Collins, Colo.), 9 May 1962, p. 2, col. 3.

304 1900 U.S. Census, Greene Co., Iowa, pop. sched., Paton Township, ED 95, p. 150, dwell. 52, fam. 52, Martin Marker household.

305 "Mrs. Griffith, Former Timnath Teacher, Dies," *Fort Collins Coloradoan*, 9 May 1962.

306 "Miss Marker's Funeral Today," *San Diego Union* (San Diego, Calif.), 11 Nov. 1964, p. 14, col. 2. California Department of Public Health, death certificate no. 64-122493 (9 Nov. 1964), Jessie Eldora Marker; Vital Records, Sacramento.

307 "Mrs. Frank Ladd is Laid to Rest in Paton," *Jefferson Bee* (Jefferson, Iowa), 27 May 1958, p. 7, col. 4.

308 Sherri Dagel, "One-Room Schoolteachers," *Goldfinch*, vol. 16 (Fall 1999): 19; imaged at the University of Iowa Libraries (pubs.lib.uiowa.edu/). "A Walk Through Iowa's One-Room Schoolhouses," Iowa Department of Education (educateiowa.gov/walk-through-iowa-s-one-room-schoolhouses).

William C. Marker

Likely Martin V. and Martha J. Marker's first child was William C. Marker who died at about age 2 on 8 March 1866.[309] He is buried in Brock Cemetery in Darke County, Ohio, next to Lyda Ellen Marker. The family tree on FamilySearch.org attributes parentage of William C. Marker to Martin V. Marker's parents, Martin Marker and Margaret (Weaver) Marker, citing Find-a-Grave.[310] The words after "son" on William C. Marker's gravestone are now unreadable, although the rest of the stone remains readable.[311] It is included in a book of cemetery inscriptions from Darke County from 1968 when presumably the gravestone was in better condition, although errors have been found in that book for other members of the Marker family.[312]

Table 2:	William C. Marker Gravestone Brock Cemetery, Darke County, Ohio	
	William C. Son [unreadable] MARKER DIED MAR 8, 1866 AGED 2 YS & 18 D'S	MARKER, William C. son of M.M. and M.J. d. 3-8-1866 ae 2y 8d
	Source: Brock Cemetery (Greenville St. Mary's Road, Darke County, Ohio; LAT/LON 40.2598818, -84.5609921), William C. Marker gravestone; read and photographed by the author, 17 May 2022.	*Source:* Anita Short and Ruth Bowers, *Cemetery Inscriptions Darke County Ohio*, 6 volumes (Greenville, Ohio: [no publisher], 1968), 2: 31.

The following evidence supports that William C. Marker was the child of Martin V. and Martha J. (Hoover) Marker and not the son of Martin and Margaret (Weaver) Marker:

---

309 Brock Cemetery (Greenville, St. Mary's Road, Darke County, Ohio; LAT/LON 40.2598818, -84.5609921), William C. Marker gravestone; read and photographed by the author, 17 May 2022. William C. Marker, d. March 8, 1866, aged 2 years & 18 d's.

310 "Family Tree," database, FamilySearch (www.familysearch.org/tree/person/details/99PL-ZGL), William C. Marker (99PL-ZGL).

311 Brock Cemetery (Greenville, St. Mary's Road, Darke Co., Ohio; LAT/LON 40.2598818, -84.5609921), William C. Marker gravestone; read and photographed by the author, 17 May 2022. Find a Grave, digital image (www.findagrave.com), memorial 138691687, William C. Marker, photograph by "DSON1492;" citing Brock Cemetery, Greenville, Darke County, Ohio.

312 "MARKER, William C. son of M.M. and M.J. d. 3–8–1866 ae 2y 8d." Short and Bowers, *Cemetery Inscriptions Darke County Ohio*, 6 vols. (Greenville, Ohio: [no publisher], 1968), 2: 31. See discussions of inscriptions for Cornelius Marker and Lyda Ellen Marker.

- Martin V. Marker and Martha J. Hoover were married on 28 May 1863.[313] Calculated from the author's reading of his gravestone, William C. Marker was born on 18 February 1864. The most probable conception dates for a child born on 18 February 1864 are 26 May 1863–30 May 1863.[314]

- If William C. Marker was not their child, Martin V. and Martha J. Marker's first known child, Emma J. Marker, was born 2 years and 8 months after they married.

- Margaret (Weaver) Marker was 46 years old when William C. Marker was born, making it less likely that she was his mother.[315]

- Martin Marker and Margaret (Weaver) Marker had two children die in infancy.[316] Those two children are accounted for: Cornelius and Lyda Ellen.[317]

- Although the inscription book lists "M. M." and M. J. Marker as the parents, the V could have been misread as an M or it could be an error either on the gravestone or in the transcription.

- Assuming that the inscription book is correct and the parents were listed by two initials, Martin and Margaret Marker did not use middle initials.[318] In contrast, Martin V. and Martha J. Marker consistently used their middle initials. Martin V. likely used a middle initial to distinguish himself from his father since they shared the same first name, Martin. And all four had names starting with M.

---

313 "Ohio, U.S., County Marriage Records, 1774–1993," database with images, no. 563, Marker-Hoover, 28 May 1863.

314 "Pregnancy Conception Calculator," Calculator.net (www.calculator.net/pregnancy-conception-calculator .htm : accessed 8 Oct. 2022).

315 For date of birth for Margaret Marker: *The History of Darke County, Ohio*, 612. Also, calculated from date of death and age, Brock Cemetery (Darke Co., Ohio), Margaret Marker gravestone. Obituary for Mrs. Margaret Marker (née Weaver), newspaper unk., 1901; in the collection of the Garst Museum, Greenville, Ohio.

316 "Death of an Old Pioneer," *Greenville Democrat*, 1 Nov. 1893.

317 See children's list for Martin Marker and Margaret (Weaver) Marker.

318 A family tree on FamilySearch lists Martin Marker with the middle initial "M," but none of the attached 16 source documents show a middle initial. "Family Tree," database, FamilySearch (www.familysearch.org /tree/person/details/99PL-ZGL), Martin M. Marker (27WN-698).

- William C. Marker's gravestone is different in appearance from Cornelius Marker's and Lyda Ellen Marker's. Their gravestones identify their parents as "M. & M. Marker."

- Johnie Marker and Stella Virginia Marker were children of Martin V. and Martha J. Marker. [319] Their gravestones, which are next to each other in Paton Township Cemetery, identify their parents as "M. V. & M. J. Marker."[320]

- Margaret (Weaver) Marker was the mother of eleven children, and those children are accounted for.[321]

- Martin V. Marker and Martha J. (Hoover) Marker were the parents of ten children—four sons and six daughters. All four sons died before July 1922.[322] If William C. was not their child, then they had an unknown son who died before 1922.

Milburn M. Marker

Martin V. and Martha J. Marker's son Milburn died a terrible death at about age 26 from ingesting carbolic acid. On 3 September 1895, Milburn was ill with typhoid fever and was staying at his brother-in-law Charles Walton's house. A nurse was hired to care for him.[323] When the nurse left the room to clear his supper dishes, Milburn drank two ounces of carbolic acid.[324] The carbolic acid, a very poisonous

---

319 For parentage of Johnie Marker: "Iowa, U.S., Births (series) 1880–1904, 1921–1944, and Delayed Births (series), 1856–1940," database with images, Ancestry (www.ancestry.com) > births and stillborn ledgers > ALL > 1882, image 879 of 2582, [white male no first name] Marker, 27 March 1882; citing State Historical Society of Iowa, Des Moines. For implied parentage of Johnie Marker: "Iowa, U.S., State Census Collection, 1836–1925," database with images, Ancestry (www.ancestry.com) > 1885 > Greene > Paton > image 13 of 29, John Marker; citing State Historical Society of Iowa, Des Moines. For parentage of Stella Virginia Marker: "Ohio, County Births, 1841–2003," digital images, FamilySearch (www.familysearch.org) > Darke > Birth registers with index 1863–1878 vol. 1 > image 149 of 342, Stella Virginia Marker, 10 June 1872; citing Darke County Probate Court, Greenville.

320 Paton Township Cemetery (U Avenue, Paton, Greene Co., Iowa; LAT/LON 42.1625453, -94.2435567), Stella Virginia Marker and Johnie Marker gravestones; read and photographed by author 7 June 2022.

321 See children's list for Martin Marker and Margaret (Weaver) Marker.

322 1900 U.S. Census, Greene Co., Iowa, pop. sched., Paton Township, ED 95, p. 150, dwelling 52, family 52, Martha J. Marker in Martin Marker household. "Martin V. Marker," *Patron Portrait* (Paton, Iowa), 3 Aug. 1922, p. 1, cols. 6–7.

323 "He Swallowed Carbolic Acid: Terrible Death of a 25-Year-Old Teacher at Paton Yesterday," *Iowa State Register* (Des Moines, Iowa), 4 Sept. 1895, p. 1, col. 3.

324 "He Swallowed Carbolic Acid: . . . ," *Iowa State Register,* 4 Sept. 1895.

chemical, had been used by the doctor to clean his instruments.[325] The doctor administered sweet oil to Milburn, to no avail. Milburn never spoke and died within a few minutes.[326] Described as a "successful and well-known school teacher" and "a young man of well balanced mind and a popular fellow,"[327] Milburn had been named the principal of Harcourt schools for the upcoming school year.[328] It was reported that a few days prior to his death, Milburn told his father that he would never recover from his illness and that the doctor could not save him.[329] Milburn's funeral was held the next day; the Reverend Joshua Jester of the Methodist Episcopal Church presided.[330]

Typhoid was a problem in Greene County, Iowa, because of swamps and poor sewage conditions; the standing water acted as a breeding ground for malaria, cholera, and typhoid.[331] "Typhoid fever was [a] frequent killer in Greene County, with a fatality rate of 30%."[332] It wasn't until 1900 that extensive tiling drainage in Greene County removed excess water, improved crops, and eliminated diseases.[333]

Typhoid is caused by bacteria. People contract it by eating or drinking food or water that has been contaminated by feces or urine that contain the bacteria. Symptoms of typhoid fever include a high fever, weakness, stomach pain, headache, diarrhea or constipation, cough, loss of appetite, and rash.[334] Without treatment, people with typhoid can become delirious.[335] Typhoid is rare today in the United

---

325 "Drank Carbolic Acid, An Awful Death at Paton," *Jefferson Bee* (Jefferson, Iowa), 5 Sept. 1895, p. 1, col. 2. "Carbolic Acid," National Cancer Institute (www.cancer.gov/publications/dictionaries/cancer-terms/def /carbolic-acid).

326 "Drank Carbolic Acid, An Awful Death at Paton," *Jefferson Bee*, 5 Sept. 1895.

327 "He Swallowed Carbolic Acid: . . . ," *Iowa State Register*, 4 Sept. 1895.

328 "Paton Pointers," *Paton Promoter* (Paton, Iowa), 7 Sept. 1895, p. 1, col. 4.

329 "Paton Pointers," *Paton Promoter*, 7 Sept. 1895.

330 For funeral date and officiant: "Drank Carbolic Acid, An Awful Death at Paton," *Jefferson Bee*, 5 Sept. 1895. For officiant's denomination: Stillman, *Past and Present of Greene County, Iowa*, 184.

331 Mikki Schwarzkopf, "The Killer Diseases of Pioneer Times," Greene County Iowa Historical Society (www .greenecountyiowahistoricalsociety.org/stories-articles/the-killer-diseases-of-pioneer-times/).

332 Schwarzkopf, "The Killer Diseases of Pioneer Times."

333 Schwarzkopf, "The Killer Diseases of Pioneer Times."

334 "Typhoid Fever and Paratyphoid Fever," Centers for Disease Control and Prevention (www.cdc.gov /typhoid-fever/symptoms.html : accessed 21 July 2022).

335 "Typhoid Fever," Mayo Clinic (www.mayoclinic.org/diseases-conditions/typhoid-fever/symptoms-causes /syc-20378661).

States thanks to chlorinated city water, the availability of vaccines, and antibiotics— none of which existed in 1895.[336]

Carbolic acid is a sweet-smelling, clear liquid.[337] As noted by a local newspaper, "It is possible that the poison was taken by mistake and not with suicidal intent."[338] Milburn may have been delirious from typhoid. The official Greene County death register reads that Milburn was about 26 years old, was a teacher, and died by "poison suicidal." Typhoid Fever was listed as a complication.[339]

Cornelius C. Marker

Less than a year after Milburn's death, Martin V. and Martha J. lost another son: Cornelius died at the age of 25. In February 1888, Cornelius Marker appeared before the "Commission of Insanity" because he had been involved in an assault. "The young man is subject to epileptic fits, which have so worked upon his mind that under excitement [he] becomes wild and absolutely dangerous in his movements." The commission considered sending Cornelius to an insane asylum in Independence, but it was full.[340] About five months later, he was admitted to the Iowa Institution for Feeble-Minded Children in Glenwood on July 23, 1888, when he was 17 years old.[341] Little is known about his time there because the chart notes no longer exist.[342]

The institution opened on 10 September 1876 with the stated intention of providing care, support, training, and instruction to feeble-minded children.[343] As of 1889, the institution cared for 432 children with a wide variety of conditions including brain abnormalities, visual impairments, and speech impediments. Seventy-six of the children had epilepsy and were kept in the "asylum division" for

336 "Typhoid Fever," Wikipedia (en.wikipedia.org/wiki/Typhoid_fever).

337 "Carbolic Acid Poisoning," Icahn School of Medicine at Mount Sinai (www.mountsinai.org/health-library /poison/carbolic-acid-poisoning).

338 "Drank Carbolic Acid, An Awful Death at Paton," *Jefferson Bee*, 5 Sept. 1895.

339 Greene County, Iowa, Death Record, vol. 2:76–77, Milburn Marker, 3 Sept. 1895; Greene County Recorder's Office, Jefferson.

340 "Pertinent Points," *Jefferson Bee* (Jefferson, Iowa), 16 Feb. 1888, p. 5, col. 3.

341 Iowa Department of Human Services, mental health records, Cornelius C. Marker (1888–1889), Glenwood Resource Center, Glenwood.

342 Teri Poe, Glenwood Resource Center, Glenwood, Iowa ([email address for private use]), to Carolyn Ladd, email, 3 Aug. 2022, "Request for Information about Cornelius Marker," Marker Genealogy Folder; privately held by Carolyn Ladd, carolynladd@comcast.net, P.O. Box 47254, Seattle, Washington 98146.

343 First Biennial Report of the Trustees, Superintendent and Treasurer of the Iowa Institution for Feeble-Minded Children at Glenwood (Des Moines, Iowa: G. H. Ragsdale, State Printer, 1877), 5 and 12.

"non-improvables." The superintendent requested that the epileptics have their own building farther away from the "education division" where 240 children who were deemed "susceptible of moral, mental, and physical improvement" received education. Children performed work at the institution that generated revenue: making bricks, sewing, and farming.[344]

A new hospital for the insane opened 15 December 1888 in Clarinda, Iowa, with 222 adult male patients. The superintendent of the hospital described the facility in very rosy terms, including that patients were encouraged to do light work in the garden or on the farm, walk outdoors, or read various periodicals provided for free by the publishers. Soon after opening its doors, however, the Iowa Hospital for the Insane at Clarinda was overcrowded.[345] The number of patients had quickly grown to over 300, and the trustees requested funds to build a "ward for violent males." As of 1 July 1891, Clarinda had 313 patients who had a wide variety of conditions;—21 of them had epilepsy,[346] one of whom was Cornelius Marker.

F. J. Bandholtz, "Iowa State Hospital for Insane, Clarinda, IA," 1909,
imaged at the Library of Congress (www.loc.gov).

On 6 September 1889, Cornelius C. Marker was discharged from the Hospital for Feeble-Minded Children and admitted as a patient at the Iowa Hospital for the Insane at Clarinda. He was 18 years old. Cornelius's admission report to Clarinda notes: "One cousin insane. Epilepsy alleged cause."[347] That cousin was likely Lavina

---

344 Seventh Biennial Report of the Trustees, Superintendent and Treasurer of the Iowa Institution for Feeble-Minded Children at Glenwood (Des Moines, Iowa: G.H. Ragsdale, State Printer, 1889), 5, 10–11, 15–16, 20–23, 24–25.

345 First Biennial Report of the Board of Trustees of the Iowa Hospital for the Insane at Clarinda, for the Fiscal Years 1888–1889 (Des Moines, Iowa: G. H. Ragsdale, State Printer, 1889), 19.

346 Second Biennial Report of the Board of Trustees of the Iowa Hospital for the Insane at Clarinda, for the Fiscal Years 1890–1891 (Des Moines, Iowa: G. H. Ragsdale, State Printer, 1891), 10, 23.

347 Iowa Department of Human Services, mental health records, Cornelius C. Marker (1889–1896), Cherokee Mental Health Institute, Cherokee.

(Marker) Lyon's son Emanuel Lyons.[348] Emanuel and Cornelius were first cousins. Cornelius's father, Martin V. Marker, and Emanuel's mother, Lavina (Marker) Lyons, were siblings.[349] Emanuel was admitted as a patient to the Iowa Hospital for the Insane at Clarinda the same year as Cornelius. Emanuel remained there for the rest of his life and died in 1918 at age 49 from tuberculosis. [350]

In the month after Cornelius was admitted to Clarinda, he had three epileptic spasms and afterwards became so "maniacal" that it was necessary to restrain him.[351] The hospital used a "camisole" (a strait jacket) and bed restraints.[352]

Five months after Cornelius Marker was admitted, the notes reflected that his physical condition was very good, but that he had been having "a number of epileptic spasms during which time he is greatly disturbed and very irritable." He destroyed the door to his bedroom and had to be restrained.[353]

In the late nineteenth century, "confinement became the preferred treatment setting for the mentally ill over the domestic setting," with many patients being confined for years.[354] Although the asylums were initially described as "healing gardens," in fact they "transformed into . . . monotonous, violent, overcrowded institution[s] for all parties involved, including superintendents, attendants, and patients."[355]

The sporadic and infrequent chart notes from Clarinda recount that Cornelius suffered from occasional seizures, was physically in good condition, but by 1894 was "growing more demented."[356] By July 1895, Cornelius's physical condition deteriorated to fair, he had frequent seizures, and he had frequent altercations with other patients. In November 1895, he was "in a very stupid condition" and was

---

348 "Death from Accident," *Carroll Times* (Carroll, Iowa), 14 March 1907, p. 1, col. 1.

349 "Death of Mrs. J. W. Lyons," *Carroll Herald* (Carroll, Iowa), 23 May 1883, p. 1, col. 5.

350 "Iowa Death Records, 1904–1951," database with images, FamilySearch (www.familysearch.org) > Film # 102902986 > image 4290 of 16956, certificate of death no. 73-2429, Emanuel R. Lyons, 21 March 1918.

351 Iowa Department of Human Services, mental health records, Cornelius C. Marker (1889–1896).

352 Second Biennial Report of the Board of Trustees of the Iowa Hospital for the Insane at Clarinda, 25–26. For definition of "camisole" as a type of restraint: Danilo Alejandro Rojas-Velasquez, "The Evolution of Restraint in American Psychiatry," Yale Medicine Thesis Digital Library (elischolar.library.yale.edu/ymtdl/2167/), 29, 30.

353 Iowa Department of Human Services, mental health records, Cornelius C. Marker.

354 "The Evolution of Restraint in American Psychiatry," 24.

355 "The Evolution of Restraint in American Psychiatry," 24.

356 Iowa Department of Human Services, mental health records, Cornelius C. Marker.

"filthy." Chart notes continue to mark a sad decline in his health. The last entry is dated 28 May 1896:

> This patient had several convulsions last night after returning and was found in an unconscious condition at 12:35. He was removed to the Infirmary but never regained consciousness and died today at 2:35 p.m. from Cerebral Hemorrhage. Post Mortem was refused. Body was sent to his father.

Cornelius's official death record lists the cause of death as a cerebral hemorrhage and epilepsy as a complication.[357] A local Greene County newspaper reported that M. V. Marker's son Neal Marker had died at Clarinda Hospital at the age of 25.[358] His death made the front page of another local paper that noted that the Marker family "seem[s] to have more than its share of afflictions this year and have the hearty sympathy of their many friends."[359] Cornelius was buried in Paton Township Cemetery next to his brother Milburn who had died just nine months before.[360]

Gravestones of Milburn and Cornelius Marker,
Paton Township Cemetery, Iowa.

357 "Iowa, U.S., Death Records, 1880–1904, 1921–1952," database with images, Ancestry (www.ancestry.com) > Registers > 1896 > image 709 of 1078, Cornelius Marker, 28 May 1896; citing State Historical Society of Iowa, State Archives, Des Moines.

358 "The News at Paton," *Jefferson Bee* (Jefferson, Iowa), 4 June 1896, p. 8, col. 6.

359 "Local and Personal," *Souvenir* (Jefferson, Iowa), 6 June 1896, p. 5, col. 4.

360 Paton Township Cemetery (U Avenue, Paton, Greene Co., Iowa; LAT/LON 42.1625453, -94.2435567).

Iowans by the Sea

In their retirement, Martin V. and Martha J. continued to move west: this time to Long Beach, California. So many Iowans moved to Long Beach in the late nineteenth and early twentieth centuries that it was called "Iowa by the Sea."[361] "Wealthy farmers first came here to retire in the 1880s and quickly spread the gospel of eternal sunshine and good living back home." The Iowa Association of Long Beach has held picnics in Southern California starting in 1887 that continue to this day.[362] The picnics feature a group sing-a-long of the "Iowa Corn Song." In 1911, a newspaper in Greene County, Iowa, ran a front-page story about the 12th Annual Iowa Picnic in Los Angeles with 35,000 in attendance, including many from Greene County who were listed by name.[363] Peak attendance at the picnic occurred in 1932 when 125,000 attended.[364]

In 1921, the Markers held a public sale of their household goods to move to Long Beach to be with their daughters Jessie and Annie Laurie.[365] Those household goods included a mahogany upright piano, an oak dresser, a sewing machine, two refrigerators, a kitchen cabinet, and a cooking range, among other items.[366]

361 Chuck Offenburger, "It's 'Iowa by the Sea'," *Des Moines Register* (Des Moines, Iowa), 10 Dec. 1994, p. T1, col. 1.

362 "121st Annual Iowa by the Sea Picnic," Iowa Association of Long Beach (www.iowabytheseapicnic.com).

363 "Iowans in California Have an Enjoyable Reunion, All Parts of Greene County Represented at the Annual Picnic Held at Los Angeles," *Jefferson Bee* (Jefferson, Iowa), 8 March 1911, p. 1, cols. 6 and 7.

364 Gustavo Arellano, "Long Beach's Iowa Picnic once drew 125,000. This year 160 attended but legacy lives on," *Los Angeles Times* (Los Angeles, Calif.), 18 Aug. 2019, [p. & col. unk.]; imaged at *Los Angeles Times* (www.latimes.com). "Iowa Corn Song," Wikipedia (en.wikipedia.org/wiki/Iowa_Corn_Song).

365 "Local and Personal," *Paton Portrait* (Paton, Iowa), 23 June 1921, p. 1, col. 2.

366 Advertisement, *Paton Portrait* (Paton, Iowa), 30 June 1921, p. 1, cols. 6–7.

Advertisement from *The Paton Portrait.*

M. V. Marker said that moving to California would make him "grow young again."[367] Martin V. and Martha J. sold their real property in Paton to their son-in-law Frank O. Ladd.[368]

On Sunday 3 July 1921, Martin V. and Martha and their daughter Jessie left by train from Grand Junction, Iowa, to travel to their new home in California.[369] Their departure was reported on the front page of the local newspaper. Two nephews, H. M. Marker and C. E. Marker, sons of Martin V.'s late brother Emanuel, came to the train station see them off.[370] Jessie had an offer for a job with the Los Angeles schools—contingent on her passing the physical exam.[371] (Presumably she passed because she became the assistant supervisor of music there.[372])

---

367 "Local and Personal," *Paton Portrait* (Paton, Iowa), 30 June 1921, p.1, col. 3.

368 "Local and Personal," *Paton Portrait.*

369 "Personal Items," *Paton Portrait* (Paton, Iowa), 7 July 1921, p. 1, col. 3.

370 "Personal Items," *Paton Portrait.* "Emanuel Marker Dead," *Jefferson Bee* (Jefferson, Iowa), 10 March 1920, p. 1, col. 4.

371 "Personal Items," *Paton Portrait.*

372 "Miss Marker's Funeral Today," *San Diego Union*, 11 Nov. 1964.

Women in California gained the right to vote in 1911, after voters approved an Equal Suffrage measure.[373] The 19th Amendment to the U.S. Constitution was ratified on 18 August 1920, granting American women the right to vote.[374] Martha registered to vote as a Democrat after moving to California.[375]

Unfortunately, Martin V. and Martha J.'s time in California was not long. Martha died on 27 January 1922 at the home of their daughter Annie Laurie in Long Beach, after suffering a stroke. Martha was just shy of 80 years old.[376] On 8 July 1922, at the age of 82, Martin V. also died at Annie Laurie's home.[377] Martin V. and Martha J. are buried together in the Sunnyside Cemetery in Long Beach, Los Angeles County, California.[378]

Gravestone of Martin V. and Martha J. Marker,
Sunnyside Cemetery, Long Beach, California.

---

373 "California Women Suffrage Centennial," State of California Secretary of State (www.sos.ca.gov/elections /celebrating-womens-suffrage/california-women-suffrage-centennial).

374 "19th Amendment to the U.S. Constitution: Women's Right to Vote," National Archives and Records Administration (www.archives.gov/milestone-documents/19th-amendment).

375 "California, U.S., Voter Registrations," database with images, Ancestry (www.ancestry.com) > Los Angeles Co. > 1922 > Roll 011; citing California State Library, Sacramento.

376 California Department of Public Health, death certificate no. 22-001890, Mrs. Martha J. Marker, 27 Jan. 1922, Bureau of Vital Statistics, Sacramento. "Death of Mrs. M. V. Marker," *Paton Portrait* (Paton, Iowa), 9 Feb. 1922, p. 2, cols. 1–2.

377 California Department of Public Health, death certificate no. 22-030921, Martin Van Buren Marker, 8 July 1922; Bureau of Vital Statistics, Sacramento.

"Martin V. Marker," *Paton Portrait* (Paton, Iowa), 13 July 1922, p. 1, col. 5.

378 Sunnyside Cemetery (1095 E. Willow Street, Long Beach, Los Angeles Co., Calif.; LAT/LON 33.80486, 118.17921), Martin V. Marker and his wife, Martha J. Marker, gravestone; read and photographed by the author, 10 Nov. 2022.

The Children of Martin Van Buren Marker and Martha Jane (Hoover) Marker

Martha Jane (Hoover) Marker was the mother of ten children, five of whom were living as of 1900.[379] When Martin Van Buren Marker died on 8 July 1922, four sons and one daughter had predeceased him; five daughters survived him.[380]

Children of Martin Van Buren Marker and Martha Jane (Hoover) Marker:

i. **WILLIAM C. MARKER,** b. prob. 28 Feb. 1864, prob. at Darke Co., Ohio; d. 8 March 1866, prob. at Darke Co.[381]

ii. **EMMA J. MARKER,** b. 29 Jan. 1866 at Darke Co.; d. 10 June 1949 at Los Angeles, Calif.;[382] m. Robert Bruton on 13 Dec. 1885 at Greene Co., Iowa.[383]

iii. **ANNIE LAURIE MARKER,** b. 4 May 1867 at Darke Co.; d. 6 July 1957, age 90, at Long Beach, Los Angeles Co., Calif.;[384] m. Charles Walton on

---

379 1900 U.S. Census, Greene Co., Iowa, pop. sched., Paton Township, ED 95, p. 150, dwelling 52, family 52, Martha J. Marker in Martin Marker household. "Iowa, U.S., Births (series) 1880–1904, 1921–1944, and Delayed Births (series), 1856–1940," database with images, Ancestry (www.ancestry.com) > births and stillborn ledgers > ALL > 1882, image 879 of 2582, [white male no first name] Marker, 27 March 1882; citing State Historical Society of Iowa; Bureau of Vital Statistics, Des Moines. This baby was the 10th child of mother, Martha Marker.

380 "Martin V. Marker," *Paton Portrait* (Paton, Iowa), 3 Aug. 1922.

381 Darke County, Ohio did not begin recording births and deaths until 1867. Alice Eicholz, ed., *The Red Book: American State, County, and Town Sources*, 3d ed. (Provo, Utah: Ancestry Publishing, 2004), 531. Brock Cemetery (Greenville, St. Mary's Road, Darke Co., Ohio; LAT/LON 40.2598818, -84.5609921), William C. Marker gravestone; read and photographed by author, 17 May 2022.

382 California Department of Public Health, death certificate no. 1901-9812, Jennie Beatrice Curtis, 10 June 1949, Bureau of Vital Statistics, Sacramento. Despite name discrepancy, the death certificate lists a date of birth as 29 Jan. 1866, place of birth as Ohio, and parents as Martin Marker and Martha Hoover.

383 "Iowa, U.S., Marriage Records, 1880–1945," database with images, Ancestry (www.ancestry.com) > 1885 > vol. 333 (Dallas-Guthrie) > image 174 of 206, Bruton-Marker, 13 Dec. 1885; citing Iowa Department of Public Health, Des Moines. The Dec. 1885 marriage record lists Emma J. Marker as 20 years old and born in "Dark" County, Ohio.

384 For parents, date and state of birth, date and location of death: California Department of Public Health, certificate of death no. 57-061633, Annie Laurie Walton, 6 July 1957; Vital Records, Sacramento. For Darke County, Ohio as specific location of birth: "Iowa, U.S., Births (series) 1880–1904, 1921–1944, and Delayed Births (series), 1856–1940," (www.ancestry.com) > Delayed Birth Records > ALL > Delayed births, no. 405001–410000, 1905–1906 > no. 407045 > image 2057 of 5017 > Affidavit of Charles Walton, 21 May 1940; citing Iowa State Archives, Des Moines.

7 Oct. 1883 at Greene Co., when she was 16 and he was a 24-year-old farmer, b. in Toronto, Canada.[385]

iv.   **MILBURN M. MARKER,** b. 1869 at Cedar Co., Iowa; d. 3 Sept. 1895 at Greene Co.[386]

v.   **CORNELIUS C. MARKER,** b. 25 Oct. 1870 at Cedar Co.;[387] d. 28 May 1896 at the Iowa Hospital for the Insane in Page Co., Iowa.[388]

vi.   **STELLA VIRGINIA MARKER,** b. 10 June 1872 at Darke Co.;[389] d. 12 Dec. 1875, abt. 3½ years old, prob. at Greene Co.[390]

385   "Iowa, U.S., Marriage Records, 1880–1945," database with images, Ancestry (www.ancestry.com) > 1884 > vol. 321 (Fayette-Humboldt) > image 53 of 155, Walton-Marker, 7 Oct. 1883; citing Iowa Department of Public Health, Des Moines. *Biographical and Historical Record of Greene and Carroll Counties, Iowa* (Chicago: Lewis Publishing, 1887), 250.

386   Cedar County, Iowa, did not begin recording births until 1880. Eicholz, *The Red Book: American State, County, and Town Sources,* 3d ed. (Provo, Utah: Ancestry Publishing, 2004), 222. For year of birth and death: Paton Township Cemetery (U Avenue, Paton, Greene County, Iowa; LAT/LON 42.1625453, -94.2435567), Milburn Marker gravestone; read and photographed by author 7 June 2022. For county and state of birth: "Iowa, U.S., State Census Collection, 1836–1925," database with images, Ancestry (www.ancestry.com) > 1885 > Paton > Greene > image 13 of 29, Milburn Marker; citing State Historical Society of Iowa, Des Moines. For death date and place: Greene County, Iowa, Death Record, vol. 2:76–77, Milburn Marker, 5 Sept. 1895; Recorder's Office, Jefferson. For father and inferred mother: 1880 U.S. Census, Greene Co., Iowa, pop. sched., Paton, ED 88, p. 14, dwelling 87, family 90, Milburn Marker in Martin Marker household. For father: "Drank Carbolic Acid, An Awful Death at Paton," *Jefferson Bee,* 5 Sept. 1895.

387   For date of birth: Iowa Department of Human Services, mental health records, Cornelius C. Marker (1888–1889), Glenwood Resource Center, Glenwood. For county of birth: "Iowa, U.S., State Census Collection, 1836–1925," database with images, Ancestry (www.ancestry.com) > 1885 > Paton > Greene > image 13 of 29, Cornelius C. Marker; citing State Historical Society of Iowa, Des Moines. For father and inferred mother: 1880 U.S. Census, Greene Co., Iowa, pop. sched., Paton, ED 88, p. 14, dwelling 87, family 90, Cornelius Marker in Martin Marker household. For father: "The News at Paton," *Jefferson Bee* (Jefferson, Iowa), 4 June 1896, p. 8, col. 6.

388   "Iowa, U.S., Death Records, 1880–1904, 1921–1952," database with images, Ancestry (www.ancestry.com) > Registers > 1896 > image 709 of 1078, Cornelius Marker, 28 May 1896; citing State Historical Society of Iowa, State Archives, Des Moines.

389   For birthdate, birthplace, and parentage: "Ohio, County Births, 1841–2003," digital images, FamilySearch (www.familysearch.org) > Darke > Birth registers with index 1863–1878, vol. 1 > image 149 of 342, Stella Virginia Marker, 10 June 1872; citing Darke County Probate Court, Greenville.

390   Paton Township Cemetery (U Avenue, Paton, Greene County, Iowa; LAT/LON 42.1625453, -94.2435567), Stella Virginia Marker gravestone; read and photographed by author 7 June 2022. No death record was found for Stella Virginia Marker. The Greene County, Iowa death register starts July 1880. Greene County, Iowa Register of Deaths & Still Births, vol. 1, p. 1; Recorder's Office, Jefferson.

vii.   **MARY THERESA MARKER,** b. 17 June 1874 at Darke Co.; d. 8 May 1962 at Fort Collins, Larimer County, Colo.;[391] m. John W. Griffith on 29 June 1907 at Colorado Springs, El Paso Co., Colo.[392]

viii.   **JESSIE ELDORA MARKER,** b. prob. 8 Nov. 1876 at Greene Co.; d. 9 Nov. 1964 at San Diego Co., Calif.[393] Jessie never married and was her own informant for her death certificate, having provided the information "pre-need." The date of birth on her death certificate of 8 Nov. 1881 conflicts with the 1880 U.S. Census that lists her as 3 years old (b. bet. 2 June 1876 and 1 June 1877), and the 1900 U.S. Census that lists her birthdate as Nov. 1876.[394] Her death certificate lists her as 83 years old at the time of her death, but she was likely 88.

+3   ix.   **HARRIET VIOLA MARKER,** b. 27 Dec. 1879 at Paton, Greene Co.; d. 22 May 1958 at Paton;[395] m. Frank Oscar Ladd on 30 March 1905 at Greene Co.[396]

---

391 "Mary Griffith, 87, Dies In Fort Collins Tuesday," *Winsor Beacon* (Winsor, Colo.), 10 May 1962, p. 1, col. 2. Mary Theresa Marker does not appear in the Darke County, Ohio, birth register index. "Ohio, County Births, 1841–2003," digital images, FamilySearch (www.familysearch.org) > Darke > Birth registers with index 1863–1878, vol. 1 > image 149 of 342; citing Darke County Probate Court, Greenville. The author does not meet the relationship requirements to order a death certificate. "Requesting a Death Certificate," Larimer County Colorado (www.larimer.org/health/health-department-general-info/birth-and-death -records/requesting-death-certificate).

392 "Colorado, U.S., Select County Marriages, 1863–2018," database with images, Ancestry (www.ancestry .com) > El Paso > 1905–1909 > image 769 of 1209, no. 4159, Griffith-Marker, 29 June 1907; citing El Paso County Recorder's Office; Colorado Springs.

393 Greene County, Iowa, did not begin recording birth records until 1880. Eicholz, *The Red Book,* 223. For parents, birth and death: California Department of Public Health, death certificate no. 64-122493 (9 Nov. 1964), Jessie Eldora Marker; Vital Records, Sacramento. For death: "Miss Marker's Funeral Today," *San Diego Union,* 11 Nov. 1964.

394 1880 U.S. Census, Greene Co., Iowa, pop. sched., Paton, ED 88, p. 14, dwelling 87, family 90, Jessie Marker in Martin Marker household. "What Day was the Census Taken Each Decade?" United States Census Bureau (www.census.gov/history/www/faqs/demographic_faqs/what_day_was_the_census_taken_each_decade .html). 1900 U.S. Census, Greene Co., Iowa, pop. sched., Paton Township, ED 95, p. 150, dwelling 52, family 52, Jessie Marker in the household of Martin Marker.

395 Iowa Department of Public Health, certificate of death no. 58-11028, Harriet Viola Ladd, 22 May 1958; Bureau of Vital Statistics, Des Moines. "Services Held for Mrs. Frank Ladd," *Paton Portrait* (Paton, Iowa), 29 May 1958, p. 1, col. 4.

396 Iowa Department of Public Health, certificate of marriage no. 37-05-813, Ladd-Marker, 30 March 1905; Bureau of Health Statistics, Des Moines. "Paton-Salem United Methodist Church," Iowa State Archives microfilm #1738301 [no p. or slide no.], Marriages, Ladd-Marker, 30 March 1905; Des Moines, Iowa.

x.   **JOHNIE M. MARKER,** b. 27 March 1882 at Greene Co.;[397] d. 5 Nov. 1888 at age abt. 6½, at Greene Co., Iowa.[398]

After Martin V. Marker purchased land in Cedar County, Iowa in 1864, Martha J. (Hoover) Marker gave birth to daughters Emma Marker in 1866 and Annie Laurie Marker in 1867 at Darke County, Ohio. Sons Milburn and Cornelius were born at Cedar County in 1869 and 1870 respectively. Martin V. purchased land in Greene County in 1872; Martha J. gave birth to daughters Stella Virginia in 1872 and Mary Theresa in 1874 at Darke County. It may be that the availability of train travel from Iowa to Darke County made it possible for Martha to give birth where she had access to better medical care or family support. Martha's mother, Ann (Curtis) Hoover, lived in Darke County in 1860 and 1870.[399] Ann died in 1881.[400]

---

397 "Iowa, U.S., Births (series) 1880–1904, 1921–1944, and Delayed Births (series), 1856–1940," database with images, Ancestry (www.ancestry.com) > births and stillborn ledgers > ALL > 1882, image 879 of 2582, [white male no first name] Marker, 27 March 1882; citing State Historical Society of Iowa, Des Moines. For implied parentage: "Iowa, U.S., State Census Collection, 1836–1925," database with images, Ancestry (www.ancestry.com) > 1885 > Greene > Paton > image 13 of 29, John Marker; citing State Historical Society of Iowa, Des Moines.

398 For birth and death dates: Paton Township Cemetery (U Avenue, Paton, Greene County, Iowa; LAT/LON 42.1625453, -94.2435567), Johnie Marker gravestone; read and photographed by author 7 June 2022. No entry was found in the Greene County register of deaths for Johnie Marker for 1888 after a page-by-page search at the Recorder's Office in Jefferson.

399 1860 U.S. Census, Darke County, Ohio, pop. sched., Wayne Township, p. 273 (handwritten), dwelling 1923, family 1928, Ann Hoover in David Hoover household; imaged at Ancestry (www.ancestry.com); citing National Archives and Records Administration microfilm publication M653, roll 956. 1870 U.S. Census, Darke County, Ohio, pop. sched., Wayne Township, p. 32 (handwritten), dwelling 243, family 243, Anna Hoover in David Hoover household; imaged at Ancestry (www.ancestry.com); citing National Archives and Records Administration microfilm publication M593, roll 1194.

400 Hoover Cemetery (Jamison Road, Darke County, Ohio; LAT/LON 40.2059924, -84.4935898), Ann Hoover gravestone; read and photographed by author 17 May 2022.

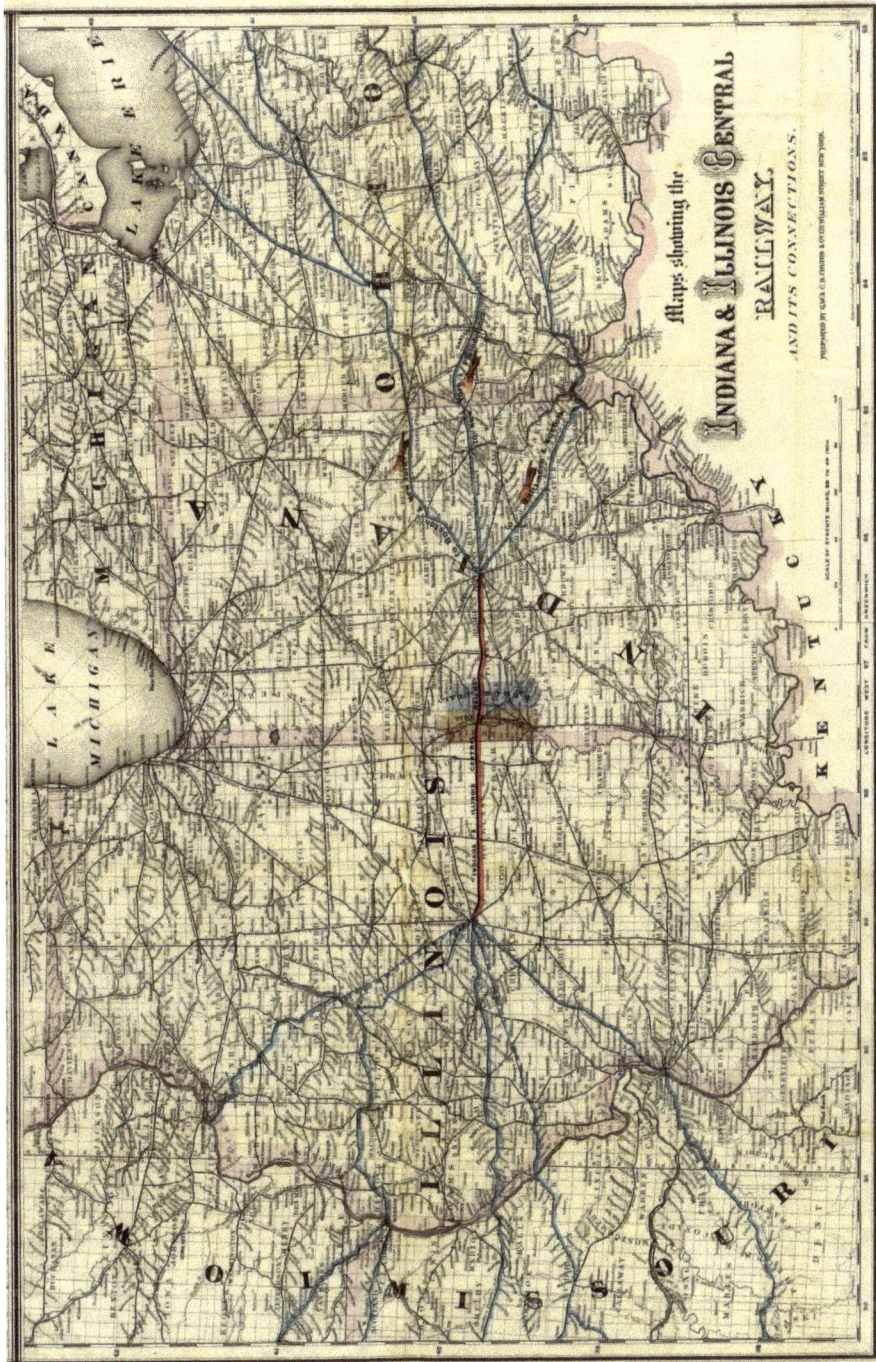

Indiana & Illinois Central Railway (New York: G. W. & C. B. Colton
& Co., 1872); imaged at Library of Congress (www.loc.gov).

Harriet Viola Marker and Frank Oscar Ladd

HARRIET VIOLA MARKER was born on 27 December 1879 in Paton, Greene County, Iowa, and died on 22 May 1958 in Paton. She was the child of Martin Van Buren Marker and Martha Jane Hoover.[401] She married **Frank Oscar Ladd** on 30 March 1905 in Paton.[402] Frank Ladd was the child of John Wesley Ladd and Elizabeth Triplett.[403]

Frank came to Paton from nearby Guthrie County at the age of 19 to work in the Harry Halloway blacksmith shop.[404] As of 1897, Frank was working as a blacksmith with his father in Paton.[405]

---

401 Iowa Department of Public Health, certificate of death no. 58-11028, Harriet Viola Ladd, 22 May 1958; Bureau of Vital Statistics, Des Moines. "Services Held for Mrs. Frank Ladd," *Paton Portrait*, 29 May 1958.

402 Iowa Department of Public Health, certificate of marriage no. 37-05-813, Ladd-Marker, 30 March 1905; Bureau of Health Statistics, Des Moines. "Paton-Salem United Methodist Church," Iowa State Archives microfilm 1738301 [no p. or slide no.], Record of Marriages, Ladd-Marker, 30 March 1905; Des Moines, Iowa.

403 Frank O. Ladd, 9 Jan. 1952, Application for Social Security Account Number (Form SS-5), Treasury Department, Internal Revenue Service. Iowa Department of Public Health, certificate of death no. 114-61-17822, Frank Oscar Ladd, 21 Aug. 1961; Bureau of Vital Statistics, Des Moines.

404 "Funeral Services for Frank O. Ladd held Thur., Aug. 24," *Jefferson Bee* (Jefferson, Iowa), 29 Aug. 1961, p. 3, cols. 6 and 7.

405 Advertisement for J. W. Ladd & Sons, *Paton Promoter*, 24 July 1897, p. 1, col. 3. For parentage and occupation: 1900 U.S. Census, Greene County, Iowa, pop. sched., Paton Township, p. 149 (stamped), enumeration district 95, sheet 32, dwelling 33, family 33, John W. Ladd household; imaged at Ancestry (www.ancestry.com: accessed 19 Sept. 2022); citing National Archives and Records Administration microfilm publication T623, roll 433.

J. W. LADD & SONS.

——THE NEW——

Blacksmith Shop

Carriage and Wagon Repairing.
Horse Shoeing,

Plow Work a Specalty.

Across street west of opera house.

PATON, - IOWA.

Advertisement from *Paton Promoter* (24 July 1897, p. 1, col. 3).

Harriet and Frank's first child, Raymond John Ladd, was born in Paton on 9 May 1906.[406] The good news of his birth—and his hefty weight of nine-and-a-half pounds—made the local newspaper. Proud father Frank Ladd handed out cigars. "Grandpa Marker and Grandpa Ladd are each wearing one of those smiles that won't come off."[407] In 1911, when Raymond was five years old, he fell while riding on the step of a car—and was run over by the back wheel of the car. Fortunately, he was not hurt, and as a local newspaper remarked: "We hope this will be a lesson to the boys to stay off the autos."[408]

Frank Ladd served as a city councilman for the town of Paton from 1903 to 1907.[409] By 1908, Frank was operating a blacksmith shop next door to his father-in-law Martin V. Marker's creamery in Paton.[410] Frank also owned "Ladd's Hall," a dance hall above the blacksmith shop that was used for a wide variety of community events,[411] including a Thanksgiving Day dinner put on by the Presbyterian ladies

---

406 Iowa Board of Public Health, certificate of birth no. 350, Raymond John Ladd, 9 May 1906; amended 23 April 1942; Bureau of Vital Statistics, Des Moines.

407 "Paton," *Grand Junction Globe* (Grand Junction, Iowa), 11 May 1906, p. 8, col. 2.

408 "The News in Greene," *Jefferson Bee* (Jefferson, Iowa), 31 May 1911, p. 8, col. 3.

409 Stillman, *Past and Present of Greene County, Iowa*, 187.

410 "$30,000 Fire at Paton," *Jefferson Bee* (Jefferson, Iowa), 16 Dec. 1908, p. 1, col. 7.

411 *Paton, The Heartland of Iowa, 1875–1975, 100 Years* (Paton, Iowa: [no pub.], 1975), 77.

for the benefit of the church;[412] a social for Valentine's Day with an opportunity to purchase a valentine and have it delivered that evening;[413] and the annual meeting of the Paton Mutual Telephone Company, when it was decided to "cut all free talk" from those who were not paying for use of the phone lines.[414]

Frank & Harriet Ladd, 1909. From the collection of John R. Ladd.

Harriet and Frank's second child, Floyd Robert Ladd, was born on 25 October 1908.[415] "Grandfather M. V. Marker, while liberally helping himself to the cigars, remarked that this was the third time during the present month of October that he has become a Grandpa."[416]

The family suffered a setback when Frank's blacksmith business was destroyed.

---

412 "The News at Paton," *Jefferson Bee* (Jefferson, Iowa), 29 Nov. 1900, p. 2, col. 2.

413 "News From Paton," *Souvenir* (Jefferson, Iowa), 14 Feb. 1903, p. 7, col. 4.

414 "Paton Items," *Grand Junction Globe* (Grand Junction, Iowa), 12 Jan. 1906, p. 1, col. 5.

415 Greene County, Iowa, Record of Births, vol. 3: 301, Floyd R. Ladd, 25 Oct. 1908; Recorder's Office, Jefferson.

416 "Paton," *Grand Junction Globe* (Grand Junction, Iowa), 30 Oct. 1908, p. 8, col. 2.

Frank Ladd and his Blacksmith Shop before the 1908 Fire.

On 10 December 1908, a spectacular fire burned the Ladd blacksmith shop to the ground along with all the other businesses on the west side of Main Street in Paton. The fire started in the Welch Sisters millinery business, likely from a defective fireplace flue. Paton did not have a fire department, so the people of the town banded together to pour water on the fire with a garden hose and buckets. The Ladd blacksmith shop was almost saved, but the water ran out and it went up in flames with the rest of the businesses.[417] According to family oral tradition, as his blacksmith shop burned to the ground, Frank Ladd carried out—by himself—through the flames a recently purchased lathe; the lathe that was so heavy it had taken three men to bring it into the shop when it was delivered.[418] Frank's losses from the fire were valued at $2,000; he had $1,600 worth of insurance.[419]

417   *Paton, The Heartland of Iowa*, 77.

418   John R. Ladd (Corvallis, Ore.), telephone interview by Carolyn Ladd, 5 June 2022; notes from interview privately held by Ladd, P.O. Box 47254, Seattle, Washington 98146. (John R. Ladd is the grandson of Frank Ladd.)

419   "$30,000 Fire at Paton," *Jefferson Bee*, 16 Dec. 1908.

Paton, Iowa, before the fire.

Paton, Iowa, after the fire, 1908.
Photos courtesy of Jim Brower and IAGenWeb Project (http://iagenweb.org/greene/)

After the fire, Frank continued to operate his blacksmith business from a barn.[420] The Ladd blacksmith shop was rebuilt in brick; before the fire it had been made of wood.[421] Frank advertised the re-opening of his shop in the newspaper in 1909:

---

420 *Paton, The Heartland of Iowa,* 40.

421 "Poem of Village Blacksmith Kept Alive in Greene County," *Jefferson Herald* (Jefferson, Iowa), 18 April 1957, p. 8, cols. 3–7.

Notice—I have my new shop completed and new machinery bought and will soon be ready and better equipped than ever to handle spring trade.

Bring in your plows, discs and machinery by the first of March and I will be ready to fix them promptly.[422]

In 1910, Frank and Harriet lived in Paton with their sons Raymond J., age 3, and Floyd R., age 15 months. Frank owned his own blacksmith shop and owned his home free of any mortgage.[423] After surviving the fire and rebuilding his business, in 1914 Frank earned $1,000 working as a blacksmith, the equivalent of about $30,000 today.[424]

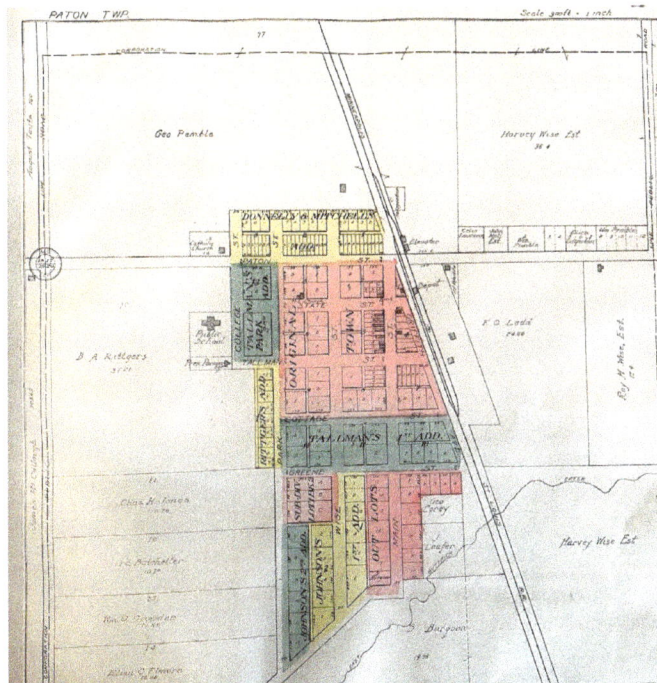

Frank O. Ladd's property in Paton, from *Standard Atlas of Greene County, Iowa* (Chicago: Geo. A. Ogle & Co., 1917), 11.

---

422 "Blacksmith's Ad," *Jefferson Herald* (Jefferson, Iowa), 26 Oct. 1954, p. 68, col. 4.

423 1910 U.S. Census, Greene County, Iowa, pop. sched., Paton Township, enumeration district 104, sheet 3A, dwelling 59, family 61, Frank O. Ladd household; imaged at Ancestry (www.ancestry.com); citing National Archives and Records Administration, microfilm publication T624, roll 403.

424 "Iowa, U.S., State Census Collection, 1836–1925," database with images, Ancestry (www.ancestry.com) > 1915 > Greene > Paton > image 476 of 988, F. O. Ladd; citing State Historical Society of Iowa, Des Moines. "Inflation Calculator," Official Data Foundation (www.in2013dollars.com).

Farmville, Virginia

In 1918, during World War I, Frank and Harriet Ladd moved their family of six from Iowa to Virginia.[425] The family now had four sons, having welcomed Wendell George Ladd, born on 30 May 1916,[426] and Chester Allen Ladd, born on 17 February 1918.[427]

A Greene County, Iowa newspaper reported: "Frank talks of making a trip east to Virginia and New York to look over some of the cheap Eastern farms."[428] Frank and his father, John W. Ladd, sold their blacksmith and wagon repair shop to a Mr. Olson from Walnut, Iowa, in March 1918.[429] An auction of Frank and Harriet's home and possessions was advertised on 16 May 1918. Items for sale included furniture, a sewing machine, an Edison Phonograph, a Coles high oven cook stove, and a soft coal magazine heater.[430] The family left Iowa for Virginia on 27 May 1918.[431] The local Paton newspaper wrote, "Frank is a good mechanic and a useful citizen and the people of Paton regret very much to see him leave and wish him the greatest measure of success in his new location."[432]

On 14 June 1918, a Virginia newspaper reported that F. O. Ladd bought a farm near Farmville, Virginia.[433] Cumberland County, Virginia, may have been an attractive location for the family based upon advertising "circulars that were sent far and wide telling in glowing terms of the prospects for settlers in the county."[434] This announcement appeared in a local Paton newspaper;

> Word from Frank O. Ladd since he reached Virginia is that he purchased a 103-acre farm including house and furniture, poultry

---

425 "Poem of Village Blacksmith Kept Alive in Greene County," *Jefferson Herald*, 18 April 1957.

426 Iowa Department of Public Health, certificate of birth no. 196, Wendell Ladd, 30 May 1916; Bureau of Vital Statistics, Des Moines.

427 Iowa Department of Public Health, certificate of birth no. 91, Chester Allen Ladd, 17 Feb. 1918; Bureau of Vital Statistics, Des Moines.

428 "Paton Portrait," *Paton Portrait*, 21 March 1918, p. 4, col. 4.

429 "J. W. & F. Ladd Sell Out," *Paton Portrait*, 14 March 1918, p. 9, col. 4.

430 "Closing-Out Sale," (advertisement), 16 May 1918, p. 4, cols. 5 and 6.

431 "Paton Portrait," *Paton Portrait* (Paton, Iowa), 30 May 1918, p. 4, col. 4.

432 "Paton Portrait," *Paton Portrait*.

433 "Personals and Briefs," *Farmville Herald* (Farmville, Va.), 14 June 1918, p. 5, col. 1.

434 Garland Evans Hopkins, *The Story of Cumberland County, Virginia* (Winchester, Va.: [no pub.], 1942), 92; imaged at FamilySearch (www.familysearch.org).

and farm machinery all for $3,000. This price seems unusually cheap to an Iowa man.[435]

The Cumberland County record of deeds actually shows that on 6 June 1918, Frank Ladd bought a 74½ acre farm for $2,000 from J. C. Mills and his wife, Anna.[436] Frank may have overpaid—J. C. Mills had purchased the property just a year prior for $1,600.[437]

By 1920, the Ladd family was back living in Iowa, and Frank was again working as a blacksmith.[438] On 28 May 1921, Frank and Harriet took out a mortgage on the Cumberland County property for $348.33, to be paid in one year with 6 percent interest.[439] The mortgage deed describes them as F. O. Ladd and Hattie Ladd his wife of Fort Dodge, Iowa (formerly of Cumberland County, Virginia).[440]

In 1929, the stock market crashed, which started The Great Depression, the largest economic crisis in American history. It lasted until 1939. Banks failed, consumer spending slowed, and people lost their jobs. "By 1933, when the Great Depression reached its lowest point, some 15 million Americans were unemployed and nearly half the country's banks had failed."[441] Farmers were impacted by falling food prices. "Farmers couldn't afford to harvest their crops and were forced to leave them rotting in the fields while people elsewhere starved."[442]

By 1935, the $348.33 mortgage on the property in Cumberland County had not been paid, and the bank called the note. Frank and Harriet were unable to pay the

---

435 "Paton Portrait," *Paton Portrait* (Paton, Iowa), 13 June 1918, p. 4, col. 3.

436 Cumberland County, Virginia, Deed Book 57:99, from J. C. Mills and his wife, Anna Mills, to Frank O. Ladd, date of document 6 June 1918, date of filing 10 June 1918; Recorder's Office, Cumberland.

437 Cumberland County, Virginia, Deed Book 55:160, from James W. Perry (widower) to J. C. Mills, date of document 9 July 1917, date of filing 13 July 1917; Recorder's Office, Cumberland.

438 1920 U.S. Census, Webster County, Iowa, pop. sched., Wahkonsa Township, enumeration district 244, sheet 3B, dwelling 51, family 57, Frank O. Ladd household; imaged at Ancestry (www.ancestry.com); citing National Archives and Records Administration microfilm publication T625, roll 518.

439 Cumberland County, Virginia, Deed Book 60:158–159, from F. O. Ladd and his wife, Hattie, Ladd to A. B. Armstrong, trustee, date of document 28 May 1921, date of filing 11 June 1921; Recorder's Office, Cumberland.

440 Cumberland County, Virginia, Deed Book 60:158–159.

441 "Great Depression History," History (www.history.com/topics/great-depression/great-depression-history).

442 "Great Depression History," History.

debt and turned the 74½-acre Virginia farm over to the bank.[443] Many others lost their farms during The Great Depression. In 1933 alone, 200,000 farms went into foreclosure in the United States.[444]

The move to Virginia and then back to Iowa seems to have had negative financial consequences for the family. In 1910, Frank and Harriet lived in a home in Paton that they owned free and clear.[445] As of 1915, they owned a home in Paton worth $2,000 with no mortgage.[446] But in 1920, after the move to Virginia and back, the family rented a home in Webster County, Iowa.[447] By 1925, they were back in Paton and lived in a home they owned worth $2,500, on which there was a $1,000 mortgage.[448]

In 1957, a Greene County, Iowa, newspaper wrote an article about Frank and Harriet and noted: "[F]or a short time during World War I they farmed in Virginia." Frank said that they found the climate pleasing in Virginia, but the land was not good for farming.[449]

Religion

Harriet's mother and Frank's parents belonged to the Methodist Church in Paton, Iowa.[450] Frank became a member of the church on 21 August 1904.[451] Harriet was also a member, although the date she became a member was not recorded.[452] Frank and Harriet were married by Eben A. Thomas, a Methodist minister, on 30 March 1905,

---

443 Cumberland County, Virginia, Deed Book 71:249, from F. O. Ladd and his wife, Hattie Ladd, to C. W. Dickoff, date of document 18 Jan. 1935, date of filing 4 Feb. 1935; Recorder's Office, Cumberland.

444 Daniel Leab, et al., eds., *The Great Depression and the New Deal, A Thematic Encyclopedia*, 2 vols. (San Diego, California: ABC-CLIO, LLC, 2010), 1:35.

445 1910 U.S. Census, Greene Co., Iowa, pop. sched., Paton Township, ED 104, sheet 3A, dwelling 59, family 61, Frank O. Ladd.

446 "Iowa, U.S., State Census Collection, 1836–1925," database with images, Ancestry (www.ancestry.com) > 1915 > Greene > Paton > image 476 of 988, F. O. Ladd; citing State Historical Society of Iowa, Des Moines.

447 1920 U.S. Census, Webster Co., Iowa, pop. sched., Wahkonsa Township, ED 244, sheet 3B, dwelling 51, family 57, Frank O. Ladd.

448 "Iowa, U.S., State Census Collection, 1836–1925," database with images, Ancestry (www.ancestry.com) > 1925 > Greene > Paton > image 25 of 111, Frank O. Ladd; citing State Historical Society of Iowa, Des Moines.

449 "Poem of Village Blacksmith Kept Alive in Greene County," *Jefferson Herald*, 18 April 1957.

450 "Paton-Salem United Methodist Church," Iowa State Archives microfilm 1738301, [no p. or slide no.], Record of Members in Full Connection, Des Moines, Iowa.

451 "Paton-Salem United Methodist Church," Iowa State Archives microfilm 1738301.

452 "Paton-Salem United Methodist Church," Iowa State Archives microfilm 1738301.

and their marriage is recorded in the records of the Paton Methodist Church.[453] Sons Raymond and Floyd were baptized at the church.[454] Frank served as a trustee at the church for 1912–1913; his father, John W. Ladd, served as a trustee and a steward during the same years.[455] In the 1915 Iowa census, Frank and Harriet and their sons Raymond and Floyd were identified as Methodist.[456] Frank Ladd remained a member of the Methodist Church.[457]

Harriet joined the Presbyterian Church while the family was living in Virginia.[458] An undated note in the records of the Paton Methodist Church noted that Harriet left for the Presbyterian Church.[459] A notation in the minutes of 25 May 1919 of the Cumberland Presbyterian Church said, "Mrs. Hattie Ladd was received on certificate from the First Methodist Church of Paton, Iowa."[460] There is no mention of other members of the Ladd family or of when she departed the church. When the family returned to Paton, Harriet joined the Paton Presbyterian Church.[461] She was active in the women's Presbyterian Missionary Society in Paton,[462] and she was elected as second vice president in 1927.[463] Presbyterian women raised money to support missionaries through fundraisers like the Birthday Offering, which started in 1922 and encouraged women to donate a penny for each year of life to support a school for girls in Japan.[464]

453 Iowa Department of Public Health, certificate of marriage no. 37-05-813, Ladd-Marker, 30 March 1905; Bureau of Health Statistics, Des Moines. "Paton-Salem United Methodist Church," Iowa State Archives microfilm 1738301, Record of Marriages [no p. or slide no.], Ladd-Marker, 30 March 1905; Des Moines, Iowa. For denomination of officiant: "E. A. Thomas, Retired Pastor, Dies in C.R.," *Gazette* (Cedar Rapids, Iowa), 28 Dec. 1945, p. 4, col. 5.

454 "Paton-Salem United Methodist Church," Iowa State Archives microfilm 1738301, [no p. or slide no.], Record of Baptisms, Raymond John Ladd & Floyd Ladd; Des Moines, Iowa.

455 "Paton-Salem United Methodist Church," Iowa State Archives microfilm 1738301.

456 "Iowa, U.S., State Census Collection, 1836–1925," database with images, Ancestry (www.ancestry.com) > 1915 > Greene > Paton > image 476 of 988, F. O. Ladd; citing State Historical Society of Iowa, Des Moines.

457 "Funeral Services for Frank O. Ladd held Thur., Aug. 24," *Jefferson Bee* (Jefferson, Iowa), 29 Aug. 1961, p. 3, cols. 6 and 7.

458 "Mrs. Frank Ladd is Laid to Rest in Paton," *Jefferson Bee*, 27 May 1958.

459 "Paton-Salem United Methodist Church," Iowa State Archives microfilm 1738301.

460 "Cumberland Presbyterian Church (Farmville, Va.), Church Records, 1797–1945," digital images, FamilySearch (www.familysearch.org) > Film# 007423290 > image 572 of 867, Minutes of Session, 25 May 1919, p. 140.

461 "Cumberland Presbyterian Church (Farmville, Va.), Church Records, 1797–1945."

462 "Enjoy Band Concerts At Paton," *The Jefferson Herald* (Jefferson, Iowa), 6 May 1926, page 6, column 5.

463 "Personal Items," *Paton Portrait* (Paton, Iowa), 10 Feb. 1927, p. 1, col. 4.

464 "History," Presbyterian Women (www.presbyterianwomen.org/who-we-are/history/).

World War II

During World War II, sons Wendell and Chester, both certified welders who had worked with their father in the Ladd blacksmith shop, put their skills to use to help in the war effort.[465] Wendell worked as a welder in Portsmouth, New Hampshire, at a naval shipyard on submarine construction.[466] As of 1940, Chester worked as a welder in the Brooklyn Navy Yards.[467]

In September 1943, Chester was drafted for military service along with fourteen other young men from Greene County.[468] He joined the Navy Seabees, serving in a Construction Battalion Maintenance Unit.[469] The Seabees took their name from the initials "C. B." for Construction Battalion.[470] They recruited skilled tradesmen so they could adapt their civilian skills to meet the needs of the military.[471] Chester served as a Shipfitter 2nd Class from September 23, 1943 until November 30, 1945, when he was honorably discharged.[472] He was stationed in Hawaii for most of his service.[473] (A shipfitter used metal sheets to repair the ship's structure and performed "forging, welding, soldering."[474])

465 "Frank Ladd—50 Years in Business," *Paton Portrait* (Paton, Iowa), 25 March 1948, p. 1, col. 5.

466 "U.S., World War II Draft Cards Young Men, 1940–1947," database with images, Ancestry (www.ancestry .com) > New Hampshire > Folger–Morancy > LaBranch, Rudolph–Lagueux, Ernest > images 1141 & 1142 of 2151, card for Wendell George Ladd, serial no. 2315, Portsmouth, New Hampshire, Board No. 19; citing National Archives and Records Administration, Records of the Selective Service System, Record Group 147. "County News, Paton," *Jefferson Bee* (Jefferson, Iowa), 16 July 1940, p. 3, cols. 2 and 3.

467 "Ladd to Federal Welding," *Paton Portrait* (Paton, Iowa), 12 Sept. 1940, p. 7, col. 4.

468 "Fifteen Accepted into Armed Services," *Jefferson Bee* (Jefferson, Iowa), 28 Sept. 1943, p. 1, col. 8.

469 Chester Allen Ladd, Notice of Separation from U.S. Naval Service (NAVPERS-553), service no. 859 68 34; World War II: Enlisted Personnel, U.S. Navy; National Personnel Records Center, St. Louis, Mo. "Iowa, U.S., World War II Bonus Case Files, 1947–1954," database with images, Ancestry (www.ancestry.com) > Claim Nos. 163995–168154 > Chester Allen Ladd, claim no. 164678. "With the Armed Forces," *Paton Portrait* (Paton, Iowa), 7 Oct. 1943, p. 1, col. 4.

470 "Seabee History: Formation of the Seabees and World War II," *Naval History and Heritage Command* (www.history.navy.mil/research/library/online-reading-room/title-list-alphabetically/s/seabee-history0 /world-war-ii.html).

471 "Seabee History: Formation of the Seabees and World War II," *Naval History and Heritage Command*.

472 Greene County, Iowa, Discharge Record no. 3, Chester Allen Ladd, serial no. 859 68 34, filed 3 Dec. 1945; Recorder's Office, Jefferson.

473 "Paton," *Jefferson Herald* (Jefferson, Iowa), 29 Nov. 1945, p. 10, col. 5.

474 "Summary of Ranks and Rates of the U.S. Navy," (Reprinted With Minor Changes From the Bureau of Naval Personnel Information Bulletin Issue of May 1943) (www.ibiblio.org/hyperwar/USN/ref/Ranks&Rates /index.html).

Over 225,000 men and women from Iowa served in the military during World War II; 8,398 Iowans died in the war.[475] Five of those Iowans were the Sullivan brothers of Waterloo, Iowa, who died on November 13, 1942 while serving on the USS *Juneau* after their ship was torpedoed and sunk in the Pacific Ocean.[476]

After the war, Wendell and Chester returned to Paton to work with their father in the blacksmith shop.[477] Over time, the blacksmithing shop morphed into welding and machining—with the advent of automobiles, very few horses were left that needed to be shoed. Frank shoed his last horse about the time of World War I.[478] Frank was able to repair automobiles and became known for his ability to fix a car called the Stanley Steamer, a steam-powered car that was manufactured from 1901 to 1924.[479] The Ladd Machine and Welding Shop in Paton provided services to farmers, auto owners, manufacturers, and garages. They had electric and acetylene welding equipment and were "scientifically equipped for all classes of machine work and welding."[480]

All three sons who worked with their father Frank in the blacksmith shop pursued metal-related careers. Wendell became the owner of the blacksmith/welding business in Paton;[481] Chester worked as an ironworker in Rockford, Illinois, for 42 years and was a member of the Iron Workers Union Local 498;[482] Raymond worked as a welding engineer at Dow Chemical in Midland, Michigan.[483]

---

475 "World War II," State Historical Society of Iowa (iowaculture.gov/goldie/at-home-expeditions/world -war-2).

476 "The Sullivan Brothers," Naval History and Heritage Command (www.history.navy.mil/browse-by-topic /disasters-and-phenomena/the-sullivan-brothers-and-the-assignment-of-family-members0.html).

477 "Wendell G. Ladd 73, Died February 12, 1990," *Paton Churdan News* (Paton, Iowa), 21 Feb. 1990, p. 4, cols. 1 and 2.

478 "Poem of Village Blacksmith Kept Alive in Greene County," *Jefferson Herald*, 18 April 1957.

479 "Frank Ladd—50 Years In Business," *Paton Portrait*, 25 March 1948. "Historic Engines—Stanley Steamer," Engine Labs (www.enginelabs.com/news/historic-engines-stanley-steamer/).

480 Advertisement, *Paton Portrait* (Paton, Iowa), 13 April 1944, p. 9, col. 3.

481 "Wendell G. Ladd 73, Died February 12, 1990," *Paton Churdan News*, 21 Feb. 1990.

482 "Chester Ladd," *Sterling Daily Gazette* (Sterling, Ill.), 14 Oct. 1998, p. A2, cols. 3 and 4.

483 For Raymond working at Dow as a chemical engineer: "Additional Paton News," *Paton Portrait* (Paton, Iowa), 29 July 1943, p. 6, col. 4. 1950 U.S Census, Midland County, Mich., pop. sched., enumeration district 56-35, sheet 28, dwelling 275, Raymond J. Ladd; citing National Archives and Records Administration, 1950 Census (1950census.archives.gov/search/). For Raymond working in the blacksmith shop with his father: "Paton," *Jefferson Herald* (Jefferson, Iowa), 12 June 1930, p. 4, col. 3.

Education

Harriet graduated from Paton School in 1896 and attended Drake University for summer school. She was a teacher for eight years prior to getting married.[484] She taught in a four-room schoolhouse in Paton for three years, and then taught in rural schools for five years.[485] Although Frank had only a 6th grade education in a rural school, he served on the school board.[486] All four of their sons completed high school.[487]

Raymond Ladd, Paton High School, 1923.

484 "Services Held for Mrs. Frank Ladd," *Paton Portrait*, 29 May 1958.

485 "Poem of Village Blacksmith Kept Alive in Greene County," *Jefferson Herald*, 18 April 1957.

486 For years of education: "Iowa, U.S., State Census Collection, 1836–1925," database with images, Ancestry (www.ancestry.com) > 1925 > Greene > Paton > image 25 of 111, Frank O. Ladd; citing State Historical Society of Iowa, Des Moines. For school board: "Frank Oscar Ladd Burial At Paton," *Paton Portrait* (Paton, Iowa), 31 Aug. 1961, p. 3, col. 3.

487 For Raymond and Floyd: "Graduates of the Paton High School," *Paton Portrait* (Paton, Iowa), 21 June 1928, p. 2, cols. 5, 6. For Wendell: "Wendell Ladd Married," *Paton Portrait* (Paton, Iowa), 5 Sept. 1940, p. 1, col. 3. For Chester: "Paton School Notes," *Jefferson Bee* (Jefferson, Iowa), 26 May 1936, p. 2, col. 2.

Son Raymond received a bachelor's degree from Iowa State University in 1933 in chemical technology.[488] Raymond paid his way through college by hauling gravel in the summers.[489] He taught for a while at Kansas State University and also worked as a chemical engineer at Dow Chemical.[490] Son Floyd Ladd studied electrical engineering at Iowa State University for a year and worked as a project engineer.[491]

Music

Harriet was known by her family to be a talented classical pianist, albeit shy about performing.[492] She performed in the Paton High School Annual Alumni Association banquet as the pianist for "Lullaby Baby."[493] She also sang in a quartet as the first alto at a benefit recital for the Ladies' Aid Society of the Methodist Episcopal Church.[494] Before they were married, Frank Ladd and Hattie Marker served together on the music committee for the Paton Day celebration.[495]

---

488 "Sixty-Second Annual Commencement," *Iowa State College of Agricultural and Mechanical Arts* (Ames, Iowa), 12 June 1933, p. 12; in the collection of the Iowa State University Archives.

489 For Raymond Ladd hauling gravel: [no title], *Jefferson Herald* (Jefferson, Iowa), 19 May 1927, p. 6, col. 5. For him paying his way through school by hauling gravel: John R. Ladd (Corvallis, Oregon), interview by Carolyn Ladd, 29 Sept. 2022; notes from interview privately held by Ladd, P.O. Box 47254, Seattle, Wash. 98146. (John R. Ladd is the son of Raymond Ladd.)

490 1950 U.S Census, Midland Co., Mich., pop. sched., ED 56-35, sheet 28, dwelling 275, Raymond J. Ladd. Michigan Department of Public Health, certificate of death no. 1033722, Raymond J. Ladd, 7 Feb. 1996; Division for Vital Records and Health Statistics, Lansing.

491 "Student Directory," Fall 1927–Winter 1928, *Iowa State College of Agricultural and Mechanical Arts* (Ames, Iowa); in the collection of the Iowa State University Archives. "Floyd R. Ladd," *Des Moines Register* (Des Moines, Iowa), 23 Oct. 1984, p. 13, col. 2.

492 Denny Ladd, Paton, Iowa ([email address for private use]), to Carolyn Ladd, email, 14 June 2022, "Ladd Family," Marker Genealogy Folder; privately held by Carolyn Ladd, carolynladd@comcast.net, P.O. Box 47254, Seattle, Washington 98146.

493 "Paton," *Jefferson Bee* (Jefferson, Iowa), 21 May 1903, p. 1, col. 3. For Paton High School Alumni Association: *Paton, the Heartland of Iowa*, 23–24.

494 "News from Paton," *Souvenir* (Jefferson, Iowa), 20 June 1903, p. 7, col. 6.

495 "Paton," *Jefferson Bee* (Jefferson, Iowa), 25 June 1903, p. 8, col. 4.

Floyd and Raymond Ladd, 1910. From the collection of John R. Ladd.

Son Chester was also a talented musician who played the trumpet. When students at a nearby high school were unable to play in a concert because of an auto accident, Chester traveled with one of his teachers to fill in. A local newspaper commented, "Chester is a remarkably good player for one of his age."[496] He was in The Paton School Orchestra and played a solo of "America" for an Armistice Day celebration.[497] In May 1931, the Paton School Orchestra traveled to Iowa City to compete in the state music contest; Chester was one of the students who made the trip.[498] While still in high school, he played trumpet solos of "Fantasia Brilliante" by Jean-Baptiste Arban with the Paton School Orchestra[499] and Felix Mendelssohn-Bartholdy's "War March of the Priests" at the Greene County Music Festival.[500]

---

496 "Personal Items," *Paton Portrait* (Paton, Iowa), 15 May 1930, p. 7, col. 6.

497 "School Notes," *Paton Portrait* (Paton, Iowa), 13 Nov. 1930, p. 7, col. 7. Armistice Day, held on Nov. 11, celebrates the end of World War I. Grun, *The Timetables of History, A Horizontal Linkage of People and Events*, 4th ed. (New York: Simon & Schuster, 2005), 472.

498 "Paton," *Jefferson Bee*, (Jefferson, Iowa) 6 May 1931, p. 7, col. 3.

499 "Musical at Paton," *Jefferson Bee* (Jefferson, Iowa), 14 March 1933, p. 2, col. 5.

500 "County Musical Festival to be Presented Here Tonight," *Jefferson Herald* (Jefferson Iowa), 19 April 1934, p. 7, col. 3.

Later Years

In 1948 at the age of 71, Frank Ladd was still working eleven-hour days in the blacksmith/welding business.[501] In 1950, he and Harriet lived north of Main Street in Paton. He earned $480 in the previous year.[502] In 1954, a note in a local newspaper said, "Mrs. Frank Ladd is the only living person today who was born, raised, married, and always lived in Paton township. She was born in December 1879."[503] At the age of 80, Frank was still working eleven-hour days, six days per week, rising at 6:00 a.m., working in his blacksmith shop with his son Wendell.[504]

Frank and Harriet were married for fifty-three years. She died on 22 May 1958 at the age of 78 after a short stay at a nursing home after a cerebral vascular accident.[505] Harriet's funeral took place at the Paton Presbyterian Church.[506] Frank died about three years later on 21 August 1961 at age 84, after a cerebral hemorrhage.[507] His funeral was held at the Methodist Church in Paton.[508] They were survived by their four sons and nine grandchildren.[509] Frank and Harriet are buried together in the Paton Township Cemetery.[510]

---

501 "Frank Ladd—50 Years in Business," *Paton Portrait*, 25 March 1948.

502 1950 U.S Census, Greene County, Iowa, pop. sched., enumeration district 37-23, sheet 11, dwelling 128, Frank Ladd; National Archives and Records Administration, 1950 Census (1950census.archives.gov /search/).

503 "Notes About Paton," *Jefferson Herald* (Jefferson, Iowa), 26 Oct. 1954, p. 29, col. 6. The newspaper erroneously omitted the time Harriet lived in Virginia during World War I.

504 "Poem of 'Village Blacksmith' Kept Alive in Greene County," *Jefferson Herald* (Jefferson, Iowa), 18 April 1957, p. 8, cols. 1–5.

505 Iowa Department of Public Health, certificate of death no. 114-58-11028, Harriet Viola Ladd, 22 May 1958; Bureau of Vital Statistics, Des Moines.

506 "Mrs. Frank Ladd is Laid to Rest in Paton," *Jefferson Bee*, 27 May 1958.

507 Iowa Department of Public Health, certificate of death no. 114-61-17822, Frank Oscar Ladd, 21 Aug. 1961; Bureau of Vital Statistics, Des Moines.

508 "Funeral Services for Frank O. Ladd held Thur., Aug. 24," *Jefferson Bee*, 29 Aug. 1961.

509 "Funeral Services for Frank O. Ladd held Thur., Aug. 24," *Jefferson Bee*, 29 Aug. 1961. "Mrs. Frank Ladd is Laid to Rest in Paton," *Jefferson Bee*, 27 May 1958.

510 Paton Township Cemetery (U Avenue, Paton, Greene Co., Iowa; LAT/LON 42.1625453°N, -94.2435567°W), Frank and "Harriett" Ladd gravestone; read and photographed by author 7 June 2022.

Gravestone of Frank and Harriet Ladd

Children of Frank Oscar Ladd and Harriet Viola Marker:

i.   **RAYMOND JOHN LADD,** b. 9 May 1906 at Paton, Greene Co., Iowa;[511] d. 7 Feb. 1996 at Midland, Midland Co., Mich.;[512] m. **HELEN MARGARET MONTAG** on 17 Sept. 1936 at West Bend, Palo Alto Co., Iowa.[513]

ii. **FLOYD ROBERT LADD,** b. 25 Oct. 1908 at Paton;[514] d. 21 Oct. 1984 at West Des Moines, Polk Co., Iowa;[515] m. (1) **IOLA IDA GUESS** on 28 July

---

511   Iowa Board of Public Health, certificate of birth no. 350, Raymond John Ladd, 9 May 1906; amended 23 April 1942; Bureau of Vital Statistics, Des Moines. Raymond John Ladd, 11 July 1939, Application for Social Security Account Number (Form SS-5), Treasury Department, Internal Revenue Service.

512   Michigan Department of Public Health, certificate of death no. 1033722, Raymond J. Ladd, 7 Feb. 1996; Division for Vital Records and Health Statistics, Lansing.

513   Iowa Department of Public Health, return of a marriage no. 674-81, Ladd-Montag, 17 Sept. 1936; Bureau of Vital Statistics, Des Moines. "Raymond Ladd Wedding," *Paton Portrait* (Paton, Iowa), 24 Sept. 1936, p. 1, col. 6.

514   Greene County, Iowa, Record of Births, vol. 3: 301, Floyd R. Ladd, 25 Oct. 1908; Recorder's Office, Jefferson.

515   Iowa Department of Public Health, certificate of death no. 114-84-020886, Floyd Robert Ladd, 21 Oct. 1984; Bureau of Vital Statistics, Des Moines. "Floyd R. Ladd," *The Des Moines Register* (Des Moines, Iowa), 23 Oct. 1984, p. 13, col. 2.

1928 at Ralston, Iowa,[516] div. 31 May 1930;[517] m. (2) **MAXINE FARBILL** on 14 Sept. 1935 at Denison, Iowa.[518]

iii. **WENDELL GEORGE LADD,** b. 30 May 1916 at Paton;[519] d. 12 Feb. 1990 at Paton;[520] m. Zeta Potter on 27 Aug. 1940 at Kittery Point, York Co., Maine.[521]

iv. **CHESTER ALLEN LADD,** b. 17 Feb. 1918 at Paton;[522] d. 13 Oct. 1998 at Sterling, Whiteside Co., Ill.;[523] m. Myrtle Miller on 23 Nov. 1940 at Adel, Dallas Co., Iowa.[524]

---

516 "Iowa, U.S., Marriage Records, 1880–1945," database with images, Ancestry (www.ancestry.com) > 1928 > vol. 1 > image 2200 of 4891, return of a marriage no. 89, Ladd-Guess, 28 July 1928; citing Iowa Department of Public Health, Des Moines. "Floyd Ladd Married," *Jefferson Herald* (Jefferson, Iowa), 9 Aug. 1928, p. 3, col. 1.

517 "Iowa, Historical Society of Iowa, Divorce Records, 1906–1937," database with images, FamilySearch (www.familysearch.org) > Film # 007422695 > image 2955 of 6160, Ladd v. Ladd, 31 May 1930; citing Historical Society of Iowa, Iowa City. "Two Divorces Granted Here, Floyd Ladd and Marie Keeling Win Freedom," *Des Moines Tribune* (Des Moines, Iowa), 31 May 1930, p. 2, col. 8.

518 "Iowa, U.S., Marriage Records, 1880–1945," database with images, Ancestry (www.ancestry.com) > 1935 > vol. 2 > image 83 of 5028, return of a marriage no. 78, Ladd-Farbill, 14 Sept. 1935; citing Iowa Department of Public Health, Des Moines. "Personals," *Jefferson Bee* (Jefferson, Iowa), 22 Oct. 1935, p. 6, col. 4.

519 Iowa Department of Public Health, certificate of birth no. 196, Wendell Ladd, 30 May 1916; Bureau of Vital Statistics, Des Moines.

520 Iowa Department of Public Health, certificate of death no. 114-1990-002401, Wendell George Ladd, 12 Feb. 1990; Bureau of Vital Statistics, Des Moines. "Wendell G. Ladd," *Des Moines Register* (Des Moines, Iowa), 14 Feb. 1990, p. 13, col. 1.

521 Maine Department of Health and Human Services, record of a marriage, Ladd-Potter, 27 Aug. 1940; Data Research and Vital Statistics, Augusta. "Wendell Ladd Married," *Paton Portrait* (Paton, Iowa), 5 Sept. 1940, p. 1, col. 3.

522 Iowa Department of Public Health, certificate of birth, no. 91, Chester Allen Ladd, 17 Feb. 1918; Bureau of Vital Statistics, Des Moines.

523 Illinois Department of Public Health, certificate of death no. 98-063420, Chester A. Ladd, 13 Oct. 1998, Springfield. "Chester Ladd," *Sterling Daily Gazette* (Sterling, Ill.), 14 Oct. 1998, p. A2, cols. 3, 4.

524 "Iowa, U.S., Marriage Records, 1880–1945," database with images, Ancestry (www.ancestry.com) > 1940 > vol. 3 > image 2741 of 5059, return of a marriage no. 25-40-197, Ladd-Miller, 23 Nov. 1940; citing Iowa Department of Public Health, Des Moines. "The News in Greene," *Jefferson Bee* (Jefferson, Iowa), 10 Dec. 1940, p. 5, col. 3.

Conclusion

THE STORY OF THE MARKER FAMILY of Maryland, Ohio, Iowa, and California is a story of faith, resilience, and persistence. Despite facing tragedy and obstacles, they persevered. Martin Van Buren Marker's dream of educating his children came true: five of his children became teachers, and a grandson graduated from college.

Frank and Harriet (Marker) Ladd family gravestones at Paton Township Cemetery, Iowa, from left to right: Wendell & Zeta Ladd, Frank & Harriet, Cornelius Marker, Milburn Marker, Johnie Marker, Stella V. Marker.

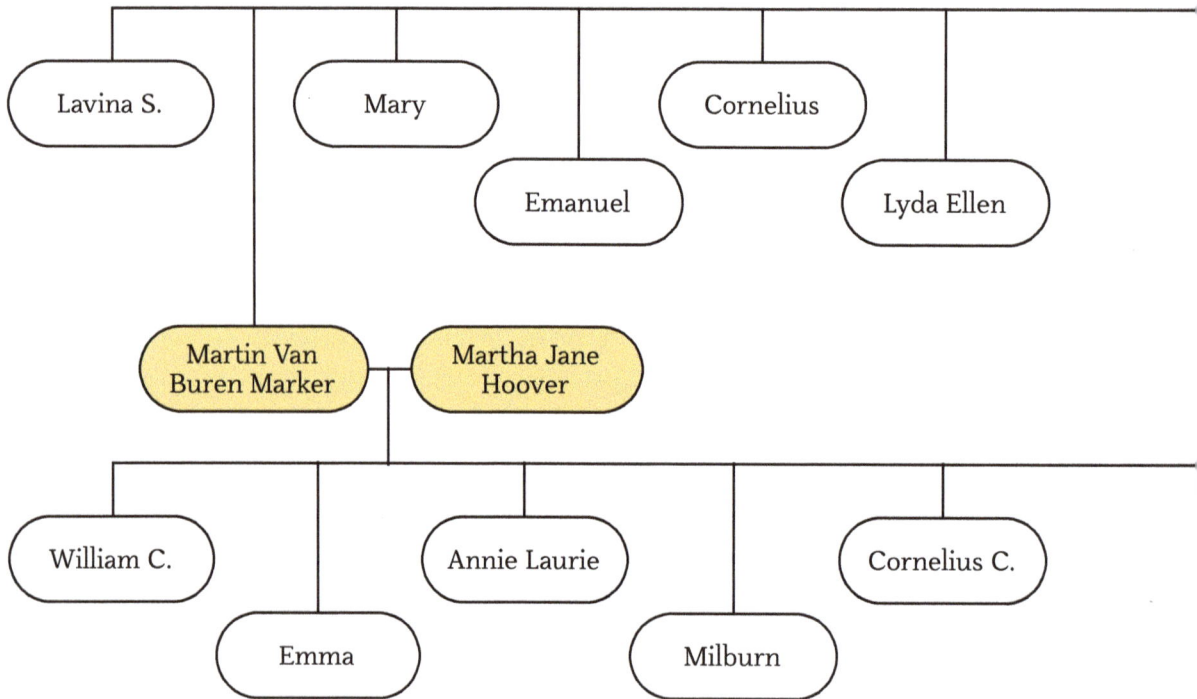

Lavina S.

Mary

Emanuel

Cornelius

Lyda Ellen

Martin Van Buren Marker

Martha Jane Hoover

William C.

Emma

Annie Laurie

Milburn

Cornelius C.

Marker Family Tree

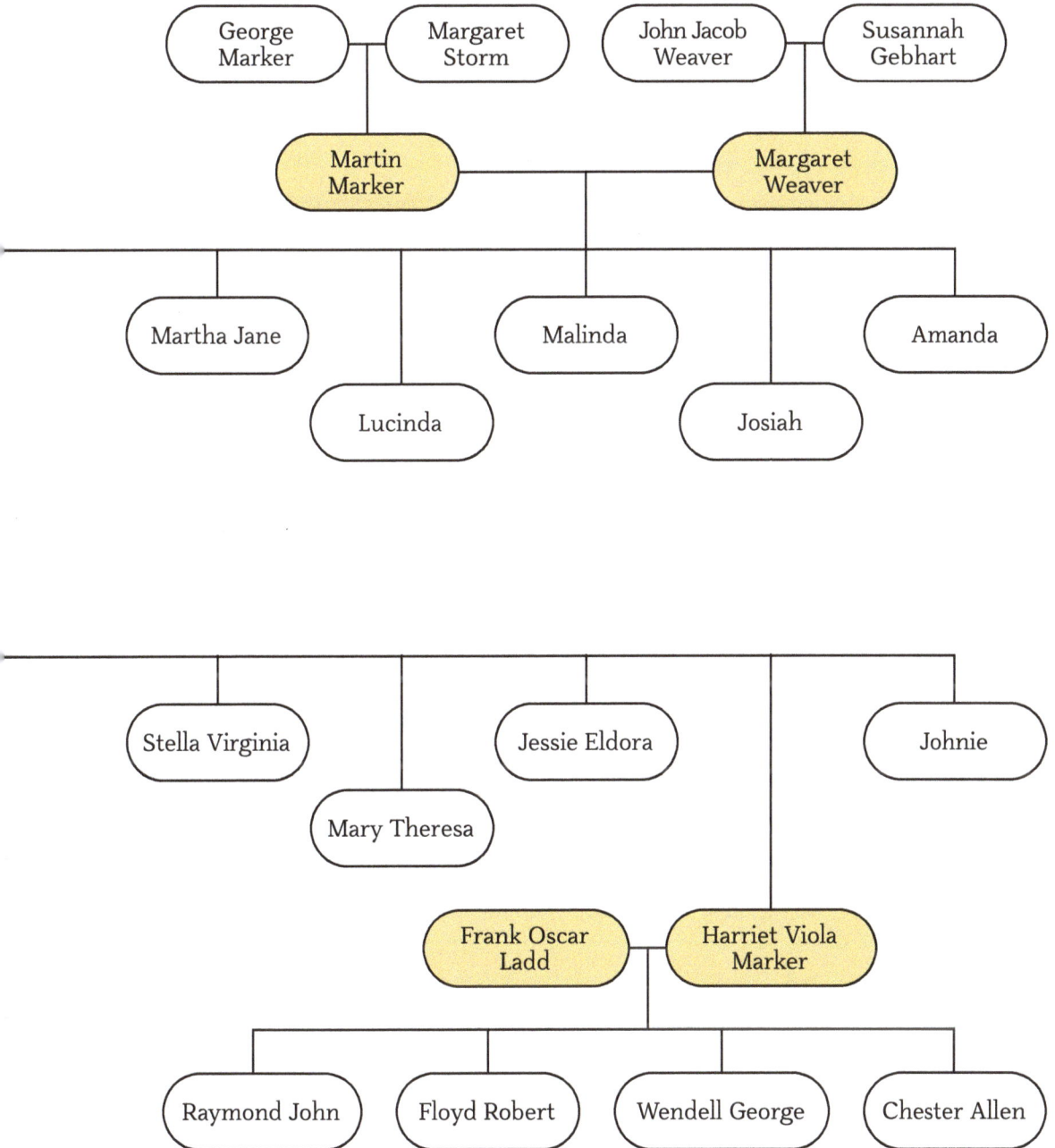

George Marker — Margaret Storm

John Jacob Weaver — Susannah Gebhart

Martin Marker — Margaret Weaver

- Martha Jane
- Lucinda
- Malinda
- Josiah
- Amanda

- Stella Virginia
- Mary Theresa
- Jessie Eldora
- Johnie

Frank Oscar Ladd — Harriet Viola Marker

- Raymond John
- Floyd Robert
- Wendell George
- Chester Allen

Index

Note: Page numbers in *italics* refer to images; page numbers ending in "t" refer to tables; and page numbers ending in "ch" refer to family tree charts.

B

Bertram
Eve Elizabeth (Weaver), 7

Boomershine
George, 18t

Bruton
Emma J. (Marker) (1866-1949), 92–93ch
birth, 57, 67, 70
childhood, 39, 43, 44
death, 67
marriage, 67
as teacher, 54
Robert, 67

Burns
Henry, 36

C

Curtis
Ann, 36, 70

F

Farbill
Maxine, 89

G

Galbraith
George, 18t

Gebhart/Gephart
George, 8
Susannah/Susanah, 7–9, 92–93ch

Gerlach/Gulach
John, 25, 35
Malinda/Melinda (Marker) (1855-1928), 23, 92–93ch
birth, 35
childhood, 16, 21
death, 35
marriage, 35
and Martin's estate, 25, 30
religion, 22

Goodall

    James W., 27–29

Griffith

    John W., 69

    Mary Theresa (Marker) (1874-1962),
        92–93ch

        birth, 69, 70

        childhood, 43, 44

        death, 69

        marriage, 69

        religion, 50

        as teacher, 54, 55

Guess

    Iola Ida, 88–89

Gulach. *See* **Gerlach/Gulach**

H

Heincke

    Henry, 1, 8, 11, 12

Helmer

    Matilda, 43

    Williamson, 39, 43

Hoover

    Ann (Curtis), 36, 70

    David, 36

    Martha Jane (1842-1922), *45*, 92–93ch

        birth, 36

        children, 39, 43, 44, 56–59, 60, 67–70

        death, 36, 66

        and education, 54

        gravestone, *66*

        marriage, 33, 36

        religion, 50–51

        retirement in California, 64–66

J

Jackson

    Richard, 18t

Jester

    Joshua, 59

L

Ladd

    Chester Allen (1918-1998), 92–93ch

        birth, 78, 89

        death, 89

        marriage, 89

        and music, 86

        occupation, 82, 83

    Elizabeth (Triplett), 72

    Floyd Robert (1908-1984), 92–93ch

        birth, 74, 88

        childhood, 77, *86*

        death, 88

        education, 85

        marriage, 88–89

        religion, 81

    Frank Oscar (1876-1961), *74,* 92–93ch

        children, 73, 78

        death, 87

        and education, 84

        gravestone, *88, 91*

        marriage, 69, 72, 80–81

        move to Virginia, 78–80

        and music, 85

        occupation, 72, 73, 74–77, 83, 87

        property, 65, 73, 75–76, *77,* 78–80

        religion, 80–81

    Harriet Viola "Hattie" (Marker) (1879-1958),
        74, 92–93ch

        birth, 69, 72

        childhood, 43, 44

        children, 73, 74, 78, 88–89

        death, 69, 72, 87

        and education, 54, 55, 84

        gravestone, *88, 91*

        marriage, 69, 72, 80–81

        and music, 85

        religion, 50, 80–81

    Helen Margaret (Montag), 88

    Iola Ida (Guess), 88–89

    John Wesley, 72, 78, 81

    Maxine (Farbill), 89

    Myrtle (Miller), 89

    Raymond John (1906-1996), 92–93ch

        birth, 73, 88

        childhood, 77, *84, 86*

        death, 88

        education, 85

marriage, 88
occupation, 83, 85
religion, 81
Wendell George (1916-1990), 92–93ch
birth, 78, 89
death, 89
gravestone, *91*
marriage, 89
occupation, 82, 83, 87
Zeta (Potter), 89, *91*

Lehman
Lawrence, 25, 27, 35
Lucinda (Marker) (1855-1937), 23, 92–93ch
birth, 35
childhood, 16, 21
death, 35
marriage, 35
and Martin's estate, 25, 30
religion, 22
visits Iowa, 50

Link
Mary, 23

Lyons
David, 23
Emanuel, 25–26, 30, 62
Isaac, 25–26, 30
Isabella/Isabelle, 22, 23, 35, 47–48
Jacob W., 25–26, 30, 33, 49
James A., 25, 30
Lavina (Marker) (1838-1883), 92–93ch
birth, 12, 33
childhood, 13, 14
children, 25, 30
death, 25, 33, 49–50
in Iowa, 46, 49
marriage, 33
Mary (Link), 23

M

Marker
Allen, 15–16
Amanda (1862-1945), 92–93ch
birth, 35
childhood, 21, 23
death, 35
marriage, 35

and Martin's estate, 25, 30
visits Iowa, 50
Annie Laurie (1867-1957), 39, 43, 64, 67–68, 70, 92–93ch
Catharine (Weaver), 7, 8, 9, 12
Catherine (_____), 17, *17*
C. E., 65
Cornelius (1848-1851), 14, 30, 31, 32, 34, 92–93ch
Cornelius C. "Neal" (1870-1896), 92–93ch
birth, 68, 70
childhood, 43, 44
death, 60, 63, 68
gravestone, *63, 91*
institutionalization, 60, 61–63
Eli/Elim, 3, 17, *17*
Eliza (_____), 15
Eliza (Miller), 34, 49
Emanuel/Manuel (1845-1920), 92–93ch
birth, 34
childhood, 14, 16, 21
death, 34, 49
marriage, 34
and Martin's estate, 25
property, 46, *46, 49*
Emma J. (1866-1949), 92–93ch
birth, 57, 67, 70
childhood, 39, 43, 44
death, 67
marriage, 67
as teacher, 54
Ezra
and brother Raymond's death, 15
and cemeteries, 24–25
and Lutheran church, 14, 21, 24
marriage, 9, 12
parents, 3
George (1780-1854), 92–93ch
birth, 3, 6
children, 2–3
death, 4
gravestone, *4*
marriage, 3, 4–5, 6
move to Ohio, 9, 11
George E. [grandchild of George], 3, 6

Marker, *continued*

Harriet Viola "Hattie" (1879-1958), *74,*
92–93ch
birth, 69, 72
childhood, 43, 44
children, 73, 74, 78, 88–89
death, 69, 72, 87
and education, 54, 55, 84
gravestone, *88, 91*
marriage, 69, 72, 80–81
and music, 85
religion, 50, 80–81

Hiram, 15

H. M., 65

Isabella/Isabelle (Lyons), 22, 23, 35, 47–48

Jacob [child of Ezra], 37, *38*

Jacob [child of George], 3

Jessie Eldora (1876-1964), 92–93ch
birth, 69
childhood, 43, 44
death, 69
move to California, 64, 65
occupation, 54, 55, 65
religion, 50, 51

Johnie M. (1882-1888), 44, 58, 70, *91,*
92–93ch

Josiah (1858-1936), 92–93ch
birth, 35
childhood, 16, 21
death, 35, 48
marriage, 22, 35
and Martin's estate, 25, 26, 48
occupation, 46, 47
property, 46, *46,* 47, *48*
religion, 47

Lavina S. (1838-1883), 92–93ch
birth, 12, 33
childhood, 13, 14
children, 25, 30
death, 25, 33, 49–50
in Iowa, 46, 49
marriage, 33

Leonard, 15, 16, 25

Lewis, 3, 5, 21–22

Lucinda (1854-1855), 15

Lucinda (1855-1937), 23, 92–93ch
birth, 35
childhood, 16, 21
death, 35

marriage, 35
and Martin's estate, 25, 30
religion, 22
visits Iowa, 50

Lyda Ellen, 30–32, *31,* 34, 92–93ch

Malinda/Melinda (1855-1928), 23, 92–93ch
birth, 35
childhood, 16, 21
death, 35
marriage, 35
and Martin's estate, 25, 30
religion, 22

Manuel (*See* Marker, Emanuel/Manuel)

Margaret (Storm) (1783-1870), 3, 4–6, *5, 6,*
92–93ch

Margaret (Weaver) (1818-1901), 92–93ch
birth, 1
children, 12, 13, 14, 16, 21, 22, 23,
30–35, 57
death, 1, 9, 23
gravestone, *24*
and J. J. Weaver's estate, 7, 20–21
marriage, 1, 11, *12*
and Martin's estate, 25, 26–27, 29–30
parents, 7–9

Margaret Catharine, 15

Martha Jane (1851-1942), 92–93ch
birth, 32, 34
childhood, 16
death, 34
marriage, 34
and Martin's estate, 25, 30
visits Iowa, 50

Martha Jane (Hoover) (1842-1922), *45,*
92–93ch
birth, 36
children, 39, 43, 44, 56–59, 60, 67–70
death, 36, 66
and education, 54
gravestone, *66*
marriage, 33, 36
religion, 50–51
retirement in California, 64–66

Martin (1815-1893), 16–23, 92–93ch
birth, 1
and brother Raymond's death, 15
childhood, 9–11
children, 12, 13, 14, 16, 21, 22, 23,
30–35, 57
death, 1, 23, 25, 48

debt to J. Goodall, 27–29
estate of, 25–27, 30, 48
gravestone, *4, 24*
and J. J. Weaver's estate, 7, 20–21
and Lutheran church, 21–22
marriage, 1, 11, *12*
move to Iowa, 16–17
occupation, 13, 14, 16, 23
parents, 2–3, 4–5, 6
property, 11, 12, 13, 14, 16–17, 21, 23, *28*
real estate investments, 18–20, *20,*
    26–27
Martin Van Buren (1840-1922), *45,* 92–93ch
birth, 13, 33, 36
childhood, 14, 16
children, 39, 43, 44, 56–59, 60, 67–70
death, 33, 36, 66
and education, 54
grandchildren, 73, 74
gravestone, *66*
land purchases by, 18t, 19, *19,* 39,
    43–44, *46*
marriage, 33, 36
and Martin's estate, 25
occupation, 39, 43–44, 45
registered for draft, 37
religion, 50–51
retirement in California, 64–66
and siblings, 46, 49, 50
Mary (1843-1936), 14, 16, 25, 30, 33, 50,
    92–93ch
Mary [child of George], 3, 15
Mary Theresa (1874-1962), 92–93ch
birth, 69, 70
childhood, 43, 44
death, 69
marriage, 69
religion, 50
as teacher, 54, 55
Milburn M. (1869-1895), 92–93ch
birth, 68, 70
childhood, 39, 43, 44
death, 58–59, 60, 68
gravestone, *63, 91*
as teacher, *52, 53,* 54
Paul, *2,* 2–3
Perry, 3, 15, 21, 22
Raymond/Raymon, 3, 15

Stella Virginia (1872-1875), 58, 68, 70, *91,*
    92–93ch
William C. (1864-1866), 30, 56–58, 56t, 67,
    92–93ch
William [child of George], 3

Maxwell
Robert, 18t

McClellan
Phebe, 39
Robert, 39

Miller
Conrad, 18t
Eliza, 34, 49
Myrtle, 89

Mills
Anna, 79
J. C., 79

Moffett
Alexander, 18t
Frances, 18t
Thomas, 18t
William, 18t

Montag
Helen Margaret, 88

Murphy
John, 25, 34
Martha Jane (Marker) (1851-1942), 92–93ch
birth, 32, 34
childhood, 16
death, 34
marriage, 34
and Martin's estate, 25, 30
visits Iowa, 50

P

Parsons
Baldwin, 18t

Potter
George, 18t
John, 18t
Zeta, 89, *91*

S

Shade
 Lucinda (Weaver), 7

Shellenberger
 Amanda (Marker), 92–93ch
  birth, 35
  childhood, 21, 23
  death, 35
  marriage, 35
  and Martin's estate, 25, 30
  visits Iowa, 50
 Rolland Ellis, 25, 35

Stine
 Hannah (Weaver), 7

Storm/Sturm
 Magdalena, 4
 Margaret (1783-1870), 3, 4–6, *5, 6*, 92–93ch
 Michael, 4

Stotler
 Christopher, 18t

T

Thomas
 Eben A., 80

Triplett
 Elizabeth, 72

W

Walton
 Annie Laurie (Marker) (1867-1957), 39, 43, 64, 67–68, 70, 92–93ch
 Charles, 67–68

Weant
 Uransey, 47, *48*

Weaver
 Anna Maria/Ann Maria/Mariah, 7, 8, 9
 Catharine, 7, 8, 9, 12
 Elias, 7
 Eve Elizabeth, 7
 Hannah, 7
 John Jacob (aka Jacob), 7–9, 20, 92–93ch
 Lucinda, 7
 Margaret (1818-1901), 92–93ch
  birth, 1
  children, 12, 13, 14, 16, 21, 22, 23, 30–35, 57
  death, 1, 9, 23
  gravestone, *24*
  and J. J. Weaver's estate, 7, 20–21
  marriage, 1, 11, *12*
  and Martin's estate, 25, 26–27, 29–30
  parents, 7–9
 Sarah, 7
 Susannah/Susanah (Gebhart/Gephart), 7–9, 92–93ch

Williams
 Mary (Marker), 3, 15
 William, 3

Windbigler
 Anna Maria/Ann Maria/Mariah (Weaver), 7, 8, 9
 Samuel, 8

Wisener
 Aaron, 25, 33
 Mary (Marker), 14, 16, 25, 30, 33, 50

Unknown Surname

Catherine, 17, *17*
Eliza, 15